Praise for *Saving Sadie*

"As an animal lover, and the owner of four fur babies of my own, plus one stray cat who found her way to my home to become a part of my family, I understood Joal Derse Dauer's love for Sadie, who she rescued from a no-kill shelter. I immediately fell in love with Sadie as you all will, too. Please, I urge all you animal lovers out there, don't walk, run to your bookstore to buy this wonderful, inspiring book. And then I urge you to do what you can for all the animals who don't have a Joal Derse Dauer to count on to give them a better life, because that's what I'm going to do as soon as I send off this testimonial."
—**Fern Michaels**, *New York Times* bestselling author

"Animals are the ultimate teachers of unconditional love. *Saving Sadie* will not only lift your spirit, open your heart, and deepen your humanness—it will make you want to tell everyone in your life to adopt, adopt, adopt! We think when we adopt a pet that we are saving *them,* but the truth is, it is they, those perfect, lovable, guardian angels in fur, who truly save *us.* This book is not only a must-read, it is a moving, undeniable, and compassionate call to action."
—**Jodee Blanco**, bullying survivor and activist and *New York Times* bestselling author of *Please Stop Laughing at Me*

Saving Sadie

How a Dog That No One Wanted Inspired the World

Joal Derse Dauer
with Elizabeth Ridley

CITADEL PRESS
Kensington Publishing Corp.
www.kensingtonbooks.com

CITADEL PRESS BOOKS are published by

Kensington Publishing Corp.
119 West 40th Street
New York, NY 10018

All Kensington titles, imprints, and distributed lines are available at special quantity discounts for bulk purchases for sales promotions, premiums, fund-raising, educational, or institutional use.

Special book excerpts or customized printings can also be created to fit specific needs. For details, write or phone the office of the Kensington sales manager: Kensington Publishing Corp., 119 West 40th Street, New York, NY 10018, attn: Sales Department; phone 1-800-221-2647.

CITADEL PRESS and the Citadel logo are Reg. U.S. Pat. & TM Off.

ISBN-13: 978-0-8065-3838-9
ISBN-10: 0-8065-3838-4

First Citadel printing: October 2017

10 9 8 7 6 5 4 3 2

Printed in the United States of America

First electronic edition: October 2017

ISBN-13: 978-0-8065-3839-6
ISBN-10: 0-8065-3839-2

*Dedicated to all the thousands of people whom
we have met
on this amazing journey. It is through your help,
love, and kindness
that we have been able to reach out and make
a difference
in the lives of so many others.*

Don't stop believing.

The greatest use of a life is to spend it on something that will outlast it.

—William James

AUTHORS' NOTE

Saving Sadie: How a Dog That No One Wanted Inspired the World is the true story of how author Joal Derse Dauer found and rescued Sadie in 2012. Some of the names have been changed to protect individuals' privacy and some characters in the story are composites based on several people.

CONTENTS

x   *Contents*

Saving
Sadie

PROLOGUE
Sadie Steals the Show

Sunday, April 24, 2016

My heart races, my throat is parched, and the butterflies in my stomach have morphed into fruit bats as the gleaming glass elevator whisks us up to the Pilot House, the elegant circular ballroom that extends from Milwaukee's Discovery World museum and aquarium out over Lake Michigan, hovering above the choppy waves. Catching my reflection in the glass, I smooth my little black dress, fluff my shoulder-length blond hair, and toss the long, pink, feather boa over my shoulder.

I glance down at my beautiful canine companion Sadie in her specially blinged-out wagon and draw strength from her calm, steady presence. What a pair we make, me in my black dress and fluorescent pink boa and she in a hand-stitched, crushed velvet bodice-and-cape dress, the skirt hemmed in bright pink rosebuds, with matching pink marabou feather wristlets and a pink-and-faux-diamond collar.

"Are we ready for this?" I ask her, genuinely concerned. She wags her tail and barks, reassuring me that we'll be fine. After four years together, we've developed a kind of emotional shorthand, a means of communication that bypasses language and allows us to connect directly, heart to heart and soul to soul.

We're on our way to a fund-raising event for GAB—Gen-

erations Against Bullying, a nonprofit anti-bullying organization for which Sadie serves as a peer "ambassa-dog," high-
lighting the connection between bullying and animal abuse
while teaching kids to become "upstanders," not bystanders,
who do the right thing when they see animals or other kids
being bullied or hurt.

Sadie and I appear at dozens of events and venues every
year, but today is special—it is Sadie's "re-birthday," the fourth
anniversary of the day we first met and she turned my life
around. Today is also special because this event will feature
the world premiere of a six-minute short film all about Sadie,
with Sadie herself hamming it up in the starring role.

The glass elevator shudders to a halt and in the moments
before the doors open, I bend down and whisper in Sadie's
ear, just as I have done so many times before, "Okay, girl, it's
show time!" She knows the drill by now, and responds with
another chirpy bark and enthusiastic wag of her tail.

The doors slide open and as I pull Sadie in her wagon out
of the elevator and along the red carpet toward the center of
the ballroom, the onslaught begins. "Sadie! Sadie! Over here!
No, over here! Can we get a photo, please? Smile, Sadie, and
say cheese!" Cameras flash, champagne flows, and the pa-
parazzi jockey for position, elbows darting and flying in
their push to get the perfect shot of Sadie, the evening's
shining star.

My head spins as I attempt to take in all the sights. The
Pilot House is draped with long, colorful sashes, festooned
with bunches of black and red balloons, and absolutely jam-
packed with the Midwest's movers and shakers, celebrities
from the political, philanthropic, and media worlds, includ-

ing Wisconsin governor and former presidential candidate Scott Walker, his wife, Tonette, longtime local TV anchorwoman Carole Meekins, and Teri Jendusa-Nicolai, domestic abuse survivor and renowned public speaker, and yet all attention is riveted to the two of us on the red carpet, and in particular Sadie, just an unassuming, medium-size, black-and-tan dog, sitting up straight and proud in a child's pull wagon, her intelligent, honey-brown eyes shining, ears flopping forward, and tail eagerly wagging. She demonstrates no fear, no nervousness, no uncertainty, even with the crowded press of people, the noise, the activity, the lights. It is as if she were born to do this, because, in fact, I believe she *was* born to do this, spreading her important message of hope and faith and perseverance, of never giving up, even in the face of overwhelming odds.

How honored and humbled I feel to be Sadie's "mom," the human she chose (and there can be no mistake about it—I did not choose her; she chose me) to be her companion, champion, advocate, and partner-in-crime for life. But how different it all seemed, four years ago tonight, when she lay lifeless and defeated in my arms, paralyzed, filthy, despondent, and incontinent, the victim of horrific abuse, and her future appeared to be measured not in years, months, or even days; mere hours remained until her scheduled rendezvous with the euthanasic needle. Isn't it incredible, how the miracle of love can so completely turn two lives around?

My reverie is interrupted by a sudden, shy-but-intent tug on my boa. I glance down to see an anxious little boy, maybe seven or eight years old, in a navy blazer, shiny new shoes, a bow tie, and thick, black-rimmed glasses. "Excuse me, but can I pet her please?" he asks, pushing up his glasses.

"Of course," I reply, taking his warm, chubby little hand in mine and guiding him to Sadie's wagon, which has been specially created for this evening, wrapped in shiny black fabric lined with rows of faux diamonds, the words *SavingSadie.com* spelled out in elegant cursive diamond lettering along either side. The crowd of adults Sadie is entertaining parts to make way for the child. A little nervous, he looks up to me for reassurance. I nod, bend, and demonstrate how to pet Sadie, moving his hand in mine over her smooth head, down her neck, and between her strong shoulders. "She's a good doggie," I say softly as Sadie gazes at the boy, slowly wagging her tail. "And she loves it when you pet her."

Sadie has a remarkable gift, a natural rapport with all living creatures, but especially with children and people with special needs. Responding to the boy's attention, she nudges him with her nose and opens her mouth, smiling her trademark tongue-wagging smile. The boy squeals with delight, stroking her head and petting her with energetic, little-boy abandon. *We may be in a room full of celebrities*, I think to myself, *but I know that it's moments like this one that Sadie and I both live for*.

Briefly leaving Sadie to her adoring fans, I work my way around the dazzlingly fancy ballroom, introducing myself, handing out business cards, and spreading our important message. I even get a photo alongside Governor Walker on the red carpet, but unfortunately the governor has a lifelong allergy to dogs so he's not able to pose with Sadie. In my few moments with the governor I take the opportunity to press him about strengthening Wisconsin's laws and punishment regarding animal abuse. Ever the politician, he agrees it's a vitally important issue and promises he'll get back to me.

Before I know it, it's time for dinner, a grand, sit-down, three-course gourmet affair consisting of a mixed mesclun salad with fresh herbs and rice wine vinaigrette, followed by an entrée of Strasbourg Chicken, a roasted chicken breast enveloped in a rich, tarragon-scented velouté sauce accompanied by pureed potatoes and French beans, and finishing with a petite honey cheesecake dessert with a sprig of fresh mint and raspberry coulis. There's no dog food for Sadie on this most special of evenings, no ordinary kibble-and-bits; no, we pull her wagon right up to our ten-person table and she sits up and joins us, human-style, listening to the conversation and following intently with her bright, soulful eyes. When we get to dessert, the whole table breaks into a rousing (if slightly off-key!) rendition of "Happy Birthday," and, to celebrate her special day, Sadie is allowed a small sample of cheesecake, which she eagerly devours, lapping it up with her tongue. *How many dogs get to do this?* I ponder. *How many dogs are blessed to have a life like Sadie's?*

They say it takes a village to raise a child; well, it takes a team, Team Sadie, to enable her, and me, to do the things we do, traveling around the country visiting schools, hospitals, libraries, pet stores, animal shelters, nursing homes, and other venues, spreading our twin messages of accepting those beings, both human and animal, who have special needs, along with pressing the need to enact stronger laws and penalties against animal abuse.

I feel especially blessed this evening to have with me several key members of Team Sadie: Jeff, my trusty dog-sitter, a soft-spoken Vietnam vet with mighty struggles of his own who nonetheless is indefatigable in caring for Sadie and my other fur babies when I am at work; my gentle and generous sister, Marnette, who traveled all the way from South Carolina to be here tonight and who was one of Sadie's earliest champions, encouraging me to keep fighting for Sadie, even when all hope appeared to be lost; Valerie, Sadie's dedicated social media guru; comedian Dobie Maxwell; friends and supporters Cindy and Brad; Dr. Jodie, the only vet willing to give Sadie a chance when other vets recommended euthanasia; and Kati, Dr. Jodie's right-hand person.

We are just finishing dessert when the lights suddenly dim and the chattering crowd of several hundred falls breathlessly silent. Dark curtains whisk elegantly across the floor-to-ceiling windows, obscuring the 360-degree view of Milwaukee's cozy harbor at twilight, as two giant screens at the front of the room flash, sputter, then flicker to blazing life. After a brief intro from the film's writer and director, GAB board chairman Bill Eisner, the somber narration begins, as the soft, gentle voice of a young woman speaks Sadie's thoughts aloud.

The other day, I heard someone talking about how lonely they were. They said they were sad, because people were making fun of them, saying really bad things about them, things that weren't even true. Things that hurt. A lot. They said that it had gotten so bad they didn't even see the point in living anymore.

Beautiful, sun-kissed images of Sadie fill the screen as the voiceover explains how Sadie's first owner shot her and left her for dead after she gave birth to a litter of puppies. *I re-*

member feeling totally alone. Abandoned. I couldn't un-
derstand how someone could be so mean to me. I hadn't
done anything to him. It was getting darker, and colder,
and even though I didn't want to leave, I could feel my
world slipping away. I started feeling sad, thinking about
all the things I would miss if my life ended that night.

What I didn't realize was that there were people who
heard the shots and came running to see what was wrong,
came to see if they could help me. They didn't want the
bully to have the last word.

I watch the screen in awe as Sadie gives Lassie a run for
her money in the acting department, re-enacting key moments from her life on film: lying prone and lifeless in a pile
of leaves with pretend blood marring her forehead; being
carried into therapy at Dr. Jodie's; swimming in the pool at
Think Pawsitive; curling up in my arms as we watch the
sunset at Bradford Beach.

The darkness of the ballroom magnifies sound, and I can
hear people sniffling, coughing, and clearing their throats
during the video's most heart-rending moments. Glancing
around me, even in the dark I catch sight of a few glimmer-
ing cheeks, and tissues surreptitiously dabbing moist eyes
as Sadie's remarkable story plays out before us.

I reach over and stroke Sadie, sitting up in her wagon beside me and intently following the action on the screen.
Sadie, everyone watching this film thinks that I rescued
you from certain death, but you and I both know that in
fact it's the other way around—you rescued me. You
changed my life, giving me meaning and purpose, open-
ing my heart to people and ideas and possibilities I could

never otherwise have imagined. And yet it was all so very different four years ago, when a brief stop at a no-kill shelter in Kenosha, Wisconsin, changed not only my life, but also the lives of thousands of other people around the world, forever.

CHAPTER ONE

A Grim Prognosis

Four years earlier: Tuesday, April 24, 2012

Having just dropped off my donation of blankets and bedding, I was in a hurry to get back on the road, but suddenly one of the dozens of dogs housed at this no-kill shelter in Kenosha, Wisconsin, caught my eye. I stopped in my tracks as my heart stuttered, my breath caught, and I took another look. I don't think I had ever seen a more pitiful creature, or a dog that had more wrong with it: sad amber eyes, defeated expression, sunken shoulders, withered back legs, wounded forehead, and dull, dirty, matted fur. The dog, along with one of the shelter's volunteers, was sitting outside in the cool, dappled shade beneath a lacy-leaved maple tree. Something in the dog's face reached out to me, drawing me closer, begging me for help. I seemed to understand instinctively that this was no ordinary dog and I needed to find out more. "What is this dog's story?" I asked the volunteer, a friendly-looking woman in her mid-forties with light brown hair.

"Her name is Sadie and she arrived here last night," she replied, then proceeded to tell me the whole story in heartbreaking detail. Sadie had been found in the hardscrabble Appalachian hills of Kentucky some weeks earlier, where, it was surmised, after giving birth to a litter of puppies she was shot between the eyes and in the back and left for dead. The strangers who found her, dazed, dehydrated, and bleeding, took her to a local vet, and when they couldn't help her there, Starfish Animal Rescue, a no-kill rescue organization based in northern Illinois, arranged to transport her to the shelter here.

"Her back legs are paralyzed," the volunteer explained. "She can't stand, she can't walk, and she's urinary and fecally incontinent." The woman shook her head sadly. She didn't have to spell out what this meant, because we both understood: Sadie, whom they estimated to be about four years old, was doomed to live out the rest of her days here, just one of many rejects, strays, and castaways, locked in a cold metal cage, until nature inevitably took its course.

"Has she been evaluated by a vet locally?" I knelt to take a closer look at Sadie. She was so skinny, so filthy and malnourished, it was difficult to make out any distinguishing characteristics, other than floppy ears, a longish snout, and, somewhere beneath the filth, black-and-tan markings. I thought she might be a hunting dog, perhaps an Australian shepherd.

"No, she hasn't seen a vet here yet," the woman replied.

"Would it be all right if I take her to a vet and have her examined?"

The volunteer looked surprised. "I'm not sure," she replied. "But we can find out."

Many times since that day, Tuesday, April 24, 2012, I have asked myself why. Why did I suddenly, out of the blue, volunteer to take Sadie, a dog I had never seen before, to the vet? I had been going to animal shelters for years, donating items and volunteering my time, and I had seen plenty of dogs, cats, and other animals with stories just as tragic as Sadie's, and yet I had never intervened like this before. Maybe it was because Sadie, even in her downcast, diminished state, reminded me of dogs I had loved and lost in the past, especially Marley, a magnificent black-and-brown Rottweiler mix, and Presley, a German shepherd mix who had died about a year earlier. Maybe if Sadie had been a Chihuahua or a pit bull, I would have just walked away, but something about Sadie's sad face, her wounded forehead, her soft, sorrowful eyes, resonated deep inside me. It was like she was trying to speak to me through her expression, as if a soul trapped somewhere deep inside of her was calling out to me for help. I reached toward Sadie and she flinched, then steadied. It was clear she didn't have the strength or the feeling in her legs to even stand up, but she did allow me to stroke her head.

On the other hand, maybe I was so drawn to Sadie not because of her pitiful state but instead because it is my nature to be "a fixer." My first impulse, when I see something broken, is to pick it up, fix it, and make it whole again. And Sadie was just about as broken as a dog could be. Then again, maybe it wasn't Sadie's desperate expression or my "fixer" persona that led me to make that choice that day: maybe it was just the magic of something that is "meant to be," the result of those unseen forces that move within and among and around us, nudging us onto the paths we were always destined to follow.

I spoke to the shelter's on-site manager and asked if I could take Sadie to the vet to see if anything could be done to help her, and in particular to get her walking again. The manager seemed surprised by my request but agreed, on one condition: that I pay the bill for the vet visit. She recommended I take Sadie to Dr. Bohdan Rudawski at the Fox Lake Animal Hospital, over the Wisconsin border in Fox Lake, Illinois. I was actually already familiar with this hospital because, coincidentally, my younger daughter, Jami-Lyn, a vet herself, had worked there with Dr. Rudawski years earlier.

Having secured the manager's permission, the volunteer helped me load Sadie into my SUV. I popped the back hatch with my remote and knelt beside Sadie, who whimpered feebly as I scooped her up in my arms. Her back legs, withered and atrophied, dangled lifelessly behind her while urine dribbled down her leg and onto my own. I also noticed, for the first time, that she had a small scrape or sore on her back paw. Frankly, she smelled terrible, from lack of care and from the mixture of dirt, urine, and feces dried and deeply matted into her fur. What was I getting myself into? And yet, even as I held her trembling body close to my chest, I felt not only her thin ribs, but also the first stirring of something like love firing inside my heart.

You are not *going to adopt this dog,* I warned myself. *You already have three fur babies at home. All you are going to do is find out whether or how Sadie might be "fixed."* And in that moment I truly believed that my head might overrule my heart, for once.

I cradled Sadie, her skinny forty-plus pounds weighing more heavily in my arms, as the volunteer smoothed and straightened the blankets that I keep in the back of my SUV for emergencies. Together we laid Sadie on top and helped her settle. I could tell she was scared, but she seemed too weak, too helpless, to offer much complaint; she simply hung her head and stared down at the blanket beneath her.

I climbed into the driver's seat and closed the door. Before I could start the engine, the volunteer motioned for me to put down the window. "Yes?" I said, leaning out on my elbow.

"Are you sure about this?" she asked skeptically, shielding her eyes from the sun.

"I'm not sure about anything," I admitted as I turned the key. "Other than the fact that this dog deserves a chance."

As we pulled out onto the two-lane country highway and past the fallow corn and cabbage fields, past the rough, weather-beaten barns and spiraling silos, I watched Sadie in my rearview mirror. She couldn't stand, but after a brief struggle she was able to sit up, pressing her black nose against the window as if desperate to scent the sweet, fresh air she had been denied so long. *That's a good girl*, I thought, cheering her in my mind. *Let's see a little bit of your fighting spirit.*

The long drive into Illinois gave me time to think about what the heck I was doing. I certainly wasn't in a position to adopt another dog, especially one with special needs. Middle-aged and on my own, I was living in Muskego, Wisconsin, a rural suburb about fifteen miles southwest of Milwaukee, and loving my work as a "transitional organization specialist," helping people to downsize, re-arrange their interiors, or prepare their homes for resale. My family included two grown-up daughters, Jo Lenette, nicknamed Joey, and Jami-Lyn, two grandchildren, one dog, and two cats.

I had trained as a dancer and later studied interior design before eventually starting my business as a transitional organization specialist. Through my business I often collected items that my clients no longer wanted or needed and then passed them along to others who could use them. In fact, it was just such a donation that had brought me to the shelter in Kenosha earlier that day. And now, here I was, racing down the I-94 interstate on a sunny spring day, with one very damaged dog huddled in the back of my SUV.

When we got to the Fox Lake Animal Hospital, I went inside, signed us in, then went back out for Sadie. When I popped open the back hatch of my SUV I was met with two things—a very guilty-looking dog with her head hung low, and the overwhelming odor of dog mess. "Oh Sadie," I said, reaching in to stroke her. "You poor girl. Don't worry— we're going to get you taken care of." Gingerly avoiding the badly soiled blankets, I once again lifted Sadie in my arms, closed the hatch, and placed Sadie down in the grass beside the parking lot. I hoped she might "do her business" here, but then I realized, to my chagrin, that I hadn't asked the people at the shelter how Sadie relieved herself. Since she couldn't stand, she also couldn't squat as a normal dog would do. If her spine was paralyzed, perhaps that meant she had no control over her bodily functions. In that case, would she spend the rest of her life in doggy diapers? And if so, would her future "forever family" willingly put up with the mess and inconvenience that entailed? I was still thinking in terms of "future" forever family at that point, because I was certain that Sadie's future family did not include me.

While we sat side by side in the grass and waited to be called in to the vet, I stroked Sadie gently, offering soft words of encouragement. I knew she didn't trust me yet, but given everything she had already endured at the hands of humans, I was amazed she let me touch her at all. As I scratched behind her ears and she let out a little low-pitched growl, I looked more closely at the dime-sized hole in her forehead where she'd been shot. The thought alone made me shiver, but I kept on petting Sadie, hoping she might somehow understand that humans could be a source of love as well as pain.

After about forty-five minutes a vet tech, a large man with kind eyes and a dazzling smile, came outside to get us, wheeling a cart. "Come on, Sadie," I coaxed her, "it's show time." The tech lifted Sadie onto the cart and together we rolled her into the bright, busy hospital and from there into an exam room, where the tech lifted Sadie up and helped me position her on the cold metal table. She must have been terrified, but Sadie just went limp, as if in surrender, as we straightened her legs and tried to make her more comfortable.

"Joal! So good to see you again." The vet, Dr. Bohdan Rudawski, already knew me as Jami-Lyn's mom, and as he bustled into the exam room, he greeted me warmly and shook my hand. About six feet tall and middle-aged with a large build, brown hair, a trim beard, and thick Eastern European accent, his whole demeanor inspired confidence.

"And who do we have here?" He gazed down at Sadie and immediately began assessing her with his eyes. I quickly explained that she was not my dog (*no, she was definitely not my dog, I kept telling myself*), but a badly injured girl that I had "borrowed" from a shelter and brought to him in hopes she could be healed.

He immediately ordered X-rays and then examined her, paying special attention to her back and hindquarters. I tried to read his face and figure out what he was thinking as he expertly moved his hands over her, pulling and prodding, this way and that, but he remained stone-faced, intense and serious. When he finished palpating Sadie's abdomen, he confirmed that she was urinary and fecally incontinent and had significant muscle and nerve damage. *Okay*, I thought, *that's bad, but she might still be fixable*.

But then the X-rays came back and the news got worse. As we suspected, a bullet was lodged in the soft tissue of Sadie's skull, between her eyes, and there was another bullet and some shrapnel in her spine, along the top of her back above her pelvis. She also had a large cyst in the middle of her tail, beneath the skin, that was concerning.

"I suspect they shot her in the head first, then shot her in the back as she turned and tried to flee. The second bullet must have stopped her cold," Dr. Rudawski surmised.

I drew a deep breath and nodded, fighting back tears. *How could anyone be so cruel to a creature so gentle, so innocent?*

Dr. Rudawski patiently explained that, given the extent of her injuries, Sadie would likely never walk or become continent again. She was not completely paralyzed; she had minimal feeling and movement in her back legs, but the damage appeared to be both extensive and permanent.

"What about surgery?" I asked hopefully. "Couldn't you operate to remove the bullets?"

He shook his head sadly. "I'm afraid not, Joal. The bullet and shrapnel in her back are too deeply embedded to even consider surgery."

"So what do you think I should do? I mean, if she were my dog, what would you recommend?" *Because Sadie is not my dog . . .*

"You could get her a cart."

"A cart?" I asked, confused.

"Yes. That way you can pull her around."

"Okay, thanks," I mumbled, too stunned to say more. It felt like someone had kicked me in the gut, but I wasn't ready to give up. I had only known this dog for a couple of hours, but I already suspected that she had something special—that she *was* something special.

I settled my bill at the front desk and again lifted Sadie in my arms, holding her even more tightly as I carried her back to my SUV and placed her inside. I settled her atop the soiled blankets and crawled in to sit beside her. We were both tired, stinky, sweaty messes. As I stroked her head I paused to cup her chin in my hand and lift her face toward mine. "Am I doing the right thing?" I asked aloud, staring into her intelligent, caramel-colored eyes that gazed back at me, fearful but also longing to trust. "Do you even *want* me to help you? Or am I only making it worse?"

Because her back was so badly injured, she could barely wag her tail, but the low whine in her throat and the quick swipe of her tongue against my palm gave me my answer: "Yes, Joal. I'm in here. Please help me to walk again."

Okay, I reasoned. *A dog is no different from a human. What do you do after you visit one doctor? You go and get a second opinion.* And I had the perfect second-opinion doctor in mind: my younger daughter, Jami-Lyn. Having previously worked with Dr. Rudawski, at this point Jami-Lyn had been working at an emergency veterinary hospital in Chicago for about five years. I climbed back into the driver's seat of my SUV, pulled out my cell phone, and quickly called Jami-Lyn. I explained where I was and that, perhaps crazily, I had assumed temporary custody of one very damaged dog. "Bring her on down," Jami-Lyn said, sounding intrigued, "and we'll take a look at her here." Even given my nature as a "fixer," it wasn't like me to spontaneously take custody of an abandoned dog and drive it halfway across the Upper Midwest seeking out veterinary advice. So I could tell by Jami-Lyn's tone she was wondering what the heck was going on.

My head was spinning during the hour-and-a-half drive from Fox Lake to Chicago's North Side. I wasn't ready to accept Dr. Rudawski's grim prognosis and still hoped against hope that something could be done to help Sadie walk again. Although I may have been rattled, Sadie seemed calm, mostly withdrawn into herself but occasionally stirring and sitting up, shoulders squared, and watching intently out the window as traffic on I-94 thickened and Chicago's dizzying skyscrapers loomed into view. I was convinced that the "real" Sadie was in there somewhere, a loving, thoughtful soul just waiting for release.

"All right, Sadie baby," I said, glancing over my shoulder as we sped down the expressway toward the Windy City, "let's keep our fingers and paws crossed for better news."

When we reached the veterinary hospital in Chicago, I quickly went in and let them know we were there. They were already waiting for us, so I went back out to the SUV and scooped Sadie up in my arms once more. She felt limp and listless, her body drained of life and hope, but suddenly she tipped her head back and rubbed my chest, then gently nuzzled my shoulder and collarbone.

Buoyed by this signal, I carried Sadie into the exam room where Jami-Lyn was waiting with a colleague, a fellow female vet who was present for the consultation. What pride and confidence I felt, placing Sadie in the capable hands of my smart, focused, gorgeous daughter, a slim, business-like blonde in her early thirties with a thousand-watt smile.

"All right, let's see what we've got here," she said as she began Sadie's physical exam. When she reached the hindquarters, her forehead furrowed with concern.

"What is it?" I asked.

"Sadie has no rectal tone whatsoever," she said sadly. "Most likely the result of the gunshot wound to her spine." Jami-Lyn concurred with Dr. Rudawski's assessment that Sadie would likely be crippled and incontinent forever.

This was no worse than Dr. Rudawski's prognosis had been, and yet it was still difficult to hear those words again. "What do you think I should do?" I asked carefully. I steeled myself for Jami-Lyn's answer as she conferred with her colleague, but nothing could have prepared me for her reply: "Realistically, we believe euthanasia is the best option," she said, followed immediately by, "If you'd like, we can do it now while you're here."

I was too shocked to respond. *Sadie is not my dog,* I thought. *I have no right to end her life.* Sensing my distress, Jami-Lyn gently took my arm and led me to the window, away from Sadie stretched out helplessly on the floor, her lifeless back legs curled in, crab-like, toward her body. "Consider the big picture, Mom," Jami-Lyn said softly as together we gazed out across the crowded parking lot. "This dog can't walk, she's urinary and fecally incontinent, and there's nothing we can do to help her. Wouldn't the kindest thing be just to end her suffering now?"

What could I say? My heart ached. Sadie seemed too beautiful, too wise and gentle a soul to simply condemn her to death. Wasn't there something, or someone, that might help? Jami-Lyn and her colleague left the room to give me some time to think. I returned to Sadie's side and gently wrapped my arms around her skinny, quivering shoulders, holding her close. "I'm so sorry," I whispered into her soft, velvety ear. "But I still believe you're a fighter. You just need a chance." I held her a while longer, petting her softly and stroking her head, until Jami-Lyn came back and asked if I was ready to proceed with the euthanasia.

"No," I told her, not even realizing I had made a decision until the words left my mouth. "I'm taking Sadie home. I understand what you're saying, and I will consider it, but I need more time. Let me call you tomorrow." I wasn't ready to let Sadie go; I was still holding out hope that there was some way to make her better and get her walking again.

As I scooped Sadie up once more and carried her back to my SUV, her weight suddenly seemed to double in my arms, and I refused to think about what it might be like to care for a dog with this level of special needs long term. I had only been Sadie's foster mom for a few hours and I was already exhausted; what would this be like twenty-four/seven? *No, Joal, don't go there*, I warned myself. *It's still possible that Sadie can be fixed. All she needs is someone to believe in her.*

It was an hour-and-forty-five-minute drive back home to

Muskego through heavy evening traffic, a drive made longer by the concern and fatigue weighing on my shoulders. Sadie must have been exhausted, too, and yet she seemed to rally, raising herself on her front legs to press her nose against the window, drawing strength and energy from the life passing by outside, so close and yet tantalizingly out of reach.

"Well, Sadie, this is it. Welcome to my humble abode," I announced when we finally arrived at my adorable old country farmhouse that had been remodeled into a chic, two-level home, nestled in a wood full of towering oak, pine, and maple trees and with a beautiful, screened-in wooden gazebo anchoring my side yard. I felt guilty, wondering if Sadie's heart beat a little faster, imagining this was her forever home. How could I explain to her that that could never be?

I left Sadie in the SUV as I went inside and was immediately overrun by my three fur babies: Sparky, my huge black Newfie-border collie mix, a big, boxy, lumbering old gal anxious to bowl me over and smother me with slobbery kisses, along with my two cats, the arch and elegant Kit Kat, a model-slim, blue-eyed, stark-white diva, and Miss Kitty, my mysterious tortoiseshell girl with vivid green eyes. The three let me know in no uncertain terms that they had missed me, and that they were hungry. "Okay, okay," I told them. "Dinner's on the way."

I wondered how they would respond to Sadie. Would they be upset or threatened by her disability, her "differentness"? Or would they welcome her into the fold? There was no point in finding out, I decided, since Sadie would not be with us for long. Instead I fed the three of them, then grabbed some more food, a water dish, and a blanket and went back out to Sadie.

I arranged Sadie's things on the ground and then lifted her out of the SUV and laid her on the cool, damp grass. I sat down beside her and stroked her head, contemplating Jami-Lyn's advice. There was no easy way to make this decision. And was it even my decision to make? Sadie seemed to relax as I stroked her, and I began to appreciate what a magnificent creature she must have been before being shot and left for dead. The fur on her back had been shaved down to the skin, allowing me to take a closer look at her injuries. I couldn't really see the bullet and shrapnel entry wounds, but there were dots where the skin had closed over. The cyst near her tail was large and could be felt beneath the skin. As I carefully stroked her forehead I could feel the bullet lodged within the tissue. Amazingly, even with all these injuries, Sadie didn't seem to be in any pain.

Spring in Wisconsin, even late April, can be cold and blustery, and snow is surprisingly common. As the sun teetered toward the horizon, a chill breeze unfurled from the woods behind us and our breaths became visible. Sadie and I huddled closer for warmth, the weight of her head resting in my lap. She and I had been sitting in the grass for over an hour. Clearly, I needed to make a decision, but for now my only decision was to put some food, water, and blankets in the garage and move Sadie there for the night. I didn't want to bring her inside the house because of her incontinence, and because I didn't want to upset or confuse Sparky, Miss Kitty, or Kit Kat. And, if I were completely honest, because I didn't want Sadie to think this was home. Her home. Our home. Her forever home. Ushering her into my home would mean ushering her into my heart, and I was still trying to convince myself that I could somehow prevent that from happening.

Even if I wasn't ready to let Sadie into my home, I also couldn't fathom leaving her outside in the elements, either. I wanted her to feel loved, even if—*especially* if—this was to be her final night on earth. At least she would fly to the angels having experienced human love firsthand.

So I settled Sadie in the detached garage, made sure she was comfortable, then went back inside and made a quick phone call to the shelter in Kenosha, letting them know that I was keeping Sadie for the night. They seemed surprised but gave their consent. After the call I slid out of my stinking, sweaty, soiled clothes, grabbed a quick shower, and fixed myself dinner. I tried to focus on my everyday tasks— cooking a meal, doing laundry, answering emails, handling follow-up calls with clients, and yet it was hard to concentrate because my mind kept returning to Sadie.

Because the garage was not attached to the house, I worried that I wouldn't hear her bark or know if she became distressed. Several times I went out to check on her, and each time I opened the door her head rose and swiveled toward me and her eyes lit up with a mixture of fear, surprise, and hope. She seemed comfortable enough, although on my second visit I noticed that she had soiled herself again. So I cleaned her up, carried her outside, and placed her in the grass, hoping she might complete her "business," but alas nothing happened. I felt sad and embarrassed for both of us that I couldn't help her with this most basic of tasks.

After I got her settled back in the garage with clean bedding, I went inside. I was so exhausted that I put on my pajamas and collapsed into bed with Sparky, Miss Kitty, and Kit Kat curling up beside me, battling each other for the curved pocket of warmth closest to Mom. I thought I'd fall asleep immediately, but every time I closed my eyes, I saw Sadie's face as I'd first seen her in the shelter, head down, chin quivering, those big brown eyes reaching out to me, begging me to help. *She's not even my dog,* I chided myself. *Why can't I get her out of my mind?*

Of course, protecting and caring for animals was nothing new for me. I had grown up in Wisconsin, with distant, difficult parents who didn't always make life pleasant for me, my older sister, Marnette, my younger sister, Leane, and my younger brother, John.

In hindsight I think that I used the love I found with animals as a substitute for what I didn't always get from the humans in my life. In any event, our home was always bursting with dogs, cats, mice, canaries, turtles, ducks, and other assorted critters. When I was six our first newly hatched duckling imprinted on me and followed me everywhere, convinced I was its "mom." By seven I had trained Rusty, our Irish setter, to sit and balance a cookie on his nose until I gave him the signal to flip it into the air and devour it.

Even at that young age I knew that animals would always play a major role in my life. But now here I was, enjoying middle age, with my two daughters grown, both of them happy and successful with terrific families and careers. I loved keeping my trim, five-foot-seven-inch dancer's body in excellent shape, and indulging my passion for classic cars and crafts and travel and skiing. Caring full-time for a disabled special-needs dog was definitely not an item on my lifetime bucket list. And yet . . . every time I closed my eyes

I saw only Sadie's sweet and patient face, looking up at me and begging for help.

After tossing and turning for several hours, at one a.m. I finally gave up, threw back the covers, and slid my legs over the side of my four-poster canopy bed. "If you can't beat 'em, join 'em," I said to Sparky, Kit Kat, and Miss Kitty, who looked confused as they stirred and blinked sleepily beside me, then promptly went back to bed. I put on my slippers, an extra layer of clothing, and my winter coat, then grabbed an extra blanket and a sleeping bag and tiptoed out to the garage. Sadie's head shot up as I entered. "It's only me, girl," I soothed her. "I thought you might like some company." She replied with a sharp little bark and a tiny-yet-determined wag of her tail.

I must admit I felt a little foolish arranging a sleeping bag and blankets and lying down to sleep on my garage floor, but Sadie needed me and that was what mattered. As I lay beside her and we snuggled closer for warmth, I spoke to her in gentle tones. "I don't have a clue what I'm doing," I admitted. "I need you to guide me. If you want my help, please tell me. And if you don't, that's okay, too. Just give me a sign."

She responded with a low, little whine that struggled to rise from the depths of her chest. Still, that was enough for now. "All right," I whispered. "Let's see what the morning brings."

After that the night grew quiet, marked only by the sound of our breathing, along with the warm, mossy odor of potting soil and the cold ache of concrete, rising from the floor beneath us to seize our joints and stiffen our bones. My eyes searched the strange, almost menacing shadows, waiting for their stark, garish forms to resolve into the more mundane shapes of a rake, a lawn mower, a deck chair, a hose. "Sadie, I want to see you run again," I whispered forcefully when I knew she was asleep. "You deserve the chance to race through the grass once more and feel the breeze move through your fur."

When I woke a few hours later the sun was up and it was clear that Sadie had soiled herself again in the night. She seemed completely mortified, with her tipped chin and downcast eyes barely able to look at me as I sat up in my sleeping bag and glanced at her. "Don't worry, girl," I said. "We'll figure this out." I stood and stretched my aching back, feeling the pain not only there but also in my arms, shoulders, neck, everywhere, not just from sleeping on the garage floor but from constantly lifting and carrying Sadie the previous day.

I opened the garage and carried Sadie outside, setting her down in the cool, crisp grass still glittering with glossy beads of morning dew. I hoped she might relieve herself, but again nothing happened. At least I had made one decision during the night: I was not going to take Sadie back to the hospital in Chicago to be euthanized. Not until we got another professional opinion, this time from Dr. Jodie.

I had been taking Sparky and my other animals to Dr. Jodie Gruenstern at the Animal Doctor Holistic Veterinary Complex for years. If anyone could offer Sadie some hope, it was Dr. Jodie. Fortunately, her clinic was almost walking distance from my house and I was able to get an appointment right away, so it was still only mid-morning when I bundled Sadie back into my SUV, drove to the clinic, and carried Sadie into one of Dr. Jodie's exam rooms. More than simply my vet, over time Dr. Jodie had become a friend, and as she entered the room I immediately felt at ease. A caring, compassionate vet committed to taking a holistic, whole-animal approach to her patients, she seemed to sense right away not only that Sadie was a special creature, but also that she was quickly becoming special to me.

Dr. Jodie's exam confirmed what the other vets had said—Sadie had virtually no rectal tone and also could not empty her bladder properly. "So her only hope then is a life-time of doggy diapers," I said sadly.

"Not necessarily," Dr. Jodie replied as her warm brown eyes brightened and she tucked a loose brown curl behind her ear. "There's a way you can help her urinate, if you're comfortable doing it." She proceeded to demonstrate for me. "You straddle her like this," she explained, standing over Sadie with Sadie centered between her legs, Sadie's head facing forward. "Then take both of your palms, with your fingers extended, lift her back end slightly upward, and gently push on both sides of her abdomen until the urine is expressed."

Then she beckoned me to come closer and try it. Sadie seemed not to mind this rather intimate indignity, and sure enough, the procedure worked. "You would need to do this for her several times a day," Dr. Jodie warned.

That thought was both hopeful and daunting. How could I, or anyone else, for that matter, who worked full-time and had a social life be available to help a dog urinate several times a day? And, of course, this still only addressed half the problem. "What about the fecal incontinence?" I asked with trepidation.

Dr. Jodie stroked her chin. "I think we can handle that through diet alone. Soften the stool and make it easier for her to relieve herself."

This was better news than I expected, but I said nothing as Dr. Jodie continued examining Sadie, listening to her heart and lungs, peering into her eyes and ears, evaluating her nerves, strength, and muscle tone, and carefully noting the position and depth of Sadie's gunshot wounds and other injuries, including the sore on her back paw and the cyst near her tail. I could see that Dr. Jodie was quickly developing a rapport with Sadie, and I appreciated how much time and attention she was lavishing on a dog that, at that point, belonged to no one. Sadie, for her part, remained a model patient, never barking, flinching, or complaining, no matter what she was asked to endure.

My heart was pounding as Dr. Jodie finished the exam and prepared to deliver her verdict. I had already explained that Dr. Rudawski recommended getting Sadie a cart while Jami-Lyn and her colleague proposed euthanasia as the best and most humane option.

"But what do *you* think?" I asked carefully. "Is there any hope for Sadie?"

"I believe we can help her," Dr. Jodie said with confidence. "I think we can make her better, improve her quality of life. I say, let's give her a chance." My spirit soared. Dr. Jodie must have seen my face light up because she quickly added, "Understand, Joal, when I say *we* can help her, I mean you and me, working together. Make no mistake, this would be a massive undertaking." I caught a flash of steel beneath the twinkle in her eye. "Few people could cope with an animal with this level of overwhelming special needs, but if anyone can handle it, Joal, I know you can. The question is, do you *want* to take this on?"

"I don't really know," I answered honestly, stroking Sadie and rubbing behind her ears, grateful she wasn't able to understand our conversation. "She's a beautiful dog and I believe she deserves the chance to walk again. But . . . it's a lot to consider. If I say yes, what would be the next steps?"

Dr. Jodie described her proposed plan. The bullet in Sadie's forehead was an immediate concern. She suggested applying a poultice several times a day to try to draw it out. She held Sadie's skull and pressed her thumbs aside the wound to demonstrate. "It appears that the bullet is lodged in the tissue beneath the skin, rather than in the bone, which is good news," she explained. "And if the poultice doesn't work, surgery to remove the bullet should be possible at some point in the near future."

"What about the bullet in her back?" I asked hopefully.

Dr. Jodie shook her head. "I'm afraid the bullet and the shrapnel in her spine are too deeply embedded to make surgical extraction an option. But I think we should consider possibly amputating Sadie's left rear leg."

This surprised me. "Really?" I asked.

"Yes," she replied. "If we can strengthen and build up her right rear leg and then amputate the left, she might be able to walk again on three legs. Let me show you what I mean." Dr. Jodie showed me how when Sadie tried to push herself upright and walk, her left rear leg automatically crossed underneath her body, like a reflex, getting in the way of the other legs and preventing her from walking. "Amputation could potentially fix this," Dr. Jodie explained.

Dr. Jodie went on to describe the overall treatment plan

as she envisioned it, encompassing therapy, holistic medications, and a special diet; a possible CT scan to further assess Sadie's injuries; swimming three times a week; acupuncture twice a week; Neuroplex and neurotrophins for nerve function; soaking in essential oils; a raw protein diet of turkey, rabbit, and beef, to minimize stool and increase muscle mass; Nature's Variety probiotics; Merrick high-quality dog food to mix with her other food; a vet wrap for the sore on her foot where it dragged when she tried to walk; oatmeal and aloe shampoo and conditioner; Nature Rich soap; and the Chinese herb Yunnan Baiyao.

Whew! Not only would the bill for all this be significant, my head spun as I tried to fathom the time, energy, and effort needed to implement such a regimen. If I did adopt Sadie, and in my mind this was still an absolute *if*, how could I possibly handle what sounded like a full-time commitment caring for such a desperately needy dog? And yet . . . here was Dr. Jodie, not making any long-term promises, but at least offering some hope. Hope. The thing I had desired most for Sadie. In Dr. Jodie I had found someone willing to give Sadie a chance.

"Look, I know this is a lot to take in," Dr. Jodie said. "Why don't you go home and take some time to think things over? If you do decide to go forward with this, come back to see me in a few days. We'll check on Sadie's progress and begin the next steps."

That sounded like a good plan. *I don't have to be Sadie's forever mom*, I reasoned. *Perhaps I could just rehab her and get her walking again.* Dr. Jodie gave me a powder and showed me how to mix it with water to make a poultice and apply it to Sadie's forehead, which I was to do twice a day in hopes of extracting the bullet. She also showed me how to clean, treat, and bandage the sore on Sadie's back paw. As I scooped up Sadie and carried her back to my SUV, she felt warm and safe in my arms, and my mood brightened. "Good girl, Sadie," I whispered in her ear. "I'm proud of you. You were an absolute star in there."

I had just settled myself behind the wheel when my cell phone rang. It was Jami-Lyn, calling from the hospital in Chicago. "Have you thought any more about the euthanasia?" she asked. My heart stopped, even though her voice was kind. "We've got an opening if you'd like to bring her in later this morning."

I knew Jami-Lyn meant well; she was concerned about me, both as a vet and as a daughter, and she perhaps understood better than anyone the heartbreak that was likely ahead of me if I decided to keep Sadie. Still, hearing her say those words was painful.

"I'm giving it a week," I said, surprising even myself with my snap decision. "I'm going to see how Sadie and I handle the next seven days. If after one week I decide that this isn't workable, I will have her euthanized. But at least I will have given Sadie the best darn week of her life."

I had tears in my eyes as I pulled out of the parking lot and onto busy Janesville Road. I glanced in the rearview mirror and saw Sadie sitting up, nose pressed to the window, watching intently as the world flew by. I knew I had some serious decisions to make. But one thing was already certain in my mind: Sadie was never, ever going back to live out her days in an animal shelter. Either I would commit to rehabbing her and getting her walking again, or I would have her put down if it became clear that her life would be too painful and too limiting for her to endure. Even so, I seriously questioned whether I had the physical, emotional, and financial resources to care for a dog that had so much wrong with her. At that moment, all Sadie and I had was a thimbleful of hope. But sometimes, even just a thimbleful of hope is enough to keep you going.

CHAPTER TWO

A Second Chance
for Sadie

That precious, trembling thimbleful of hope that I clung to so desperately as we pulled out of Dr. Jodie's parking lot was sorely tested during my first few exhausting days as Sadie's temporary foster mom. Sadie was clearly deeply traumatized by everything she had experienced during and after being shot, but that trauma showed itself not in fear or cowering or aggressively acting out but instead in almost complete passivity. It broke my heart to see Sadie just "sitting there," withdrawn into herself, not complaining about anything, but also not willing to engage, with me or with her surroundings. She watched, as if from a distance—a spectator, not a participant, in life.

Once settled at home I kept searching for glimpses of the "real" Sadie I had seen earlier, albeit briefly, at the shelter and afterward. What had become of that bright, energetic, affectionate dog who was trapped inside a mangled body and just itching to get out? I wondered, had Sadie lost the will to live? Had she suffered brain damage from the bullet to her forehead? The X-rays suggested the bullet was lodged in the soft tissue and hadn't breached the skull, but we couldn't yet be certain of the extent of the damage. I had wanted to save Sadie from the moment I first laid eyes on her. But was there even a dog inside there somewhere worth saving? Suddenly I was forced to ask myself some really difficult and painful questions.

After that first slightly hopeful appointment with Dr. Jodie on Wednesday, I took off work Thursday and Friday to spend time with Sadie, getting to know her better and figuring out whether some kind of long-term rehabilitation plan to get her walking again would even be feasible. In my mind it was important that Sadie show at least some progress, physically, mentally, emotionally, psychologically, during that first week in order to justify either of us sticking with this long term. I knew how cruel and selfish it would be to ask a beautiful, intelligent, dignified hunting dog like Sadie to spend the rest of her life incontinent, slowly and painfully staggering forward as she dragged her lifeless back legs behind her like so much dead weight. That was clearly not the future I envisioned for her or the future that she deserved.

In truth, Sadie's immediate needs were so immense that I often feared we wouldn't make it through the full week I had impulsively promised her after our appointment with Dr. Jodie. Jami-Lyn's recommendation of euthanasia, which I knew sprang only from love and compassion, continued to haunt me, and in the back of my mind I understood there was an "easy" way out, if I so chose. After all, I kept reminding myself, Sadie was not "my" dog but just a stray that I had "borrowed" in the hopes of helping her heal. But, on the other hand, I was also still staunchly in "fixer mode," waiting for the breakthrough that would convince me that Sadie not only wanted to, but *would* walk again.

Positive person that I am, I tried not to think about the clock ticking ominously in the background and casting a shadow over our days, a steady, ever-present, metronomic beat reminding me that when the week was over, I would have to make a life-or-death decision about Sadie's future. In the meantime, there were more practical problems to attend to, particularly concerning bathroom issues.

The technique Dr. Jodie recommended for emptying Sadie's bladder was only partially successful. When I took Sadie outside and helped her "go," centering her between my legs and pressing either side of her abdomen, a strong, steady stream of urine emerged, but she still had a lot of issues with leakage between "bathroom visits." I couldn't very well continue sleeping outside beside her in the garage, but I also could not have her leaking all over my carpets and furniture, so it appeared that diapers were, regrettably, the only answer. A quick online search showed that doggy diapers, while readily available, were also much more expensive than human baby diapers.

A 12-pack of female doggy diapers cost $9.97, or about eighty-three cents per diaper, while a 44-pack of toddler diapers (the size Sadie would need) cost $8.97, which works out to about twenty cents per diaper. The sixty-three-cent difference between a baby diaper and a doggy diaper might not seem like much, but when I did a rough calculation of how many diapers Sadie would likely go through in a typical day (quite a few!), the difference was significant.

"Okay, Sadie," I said, as her passive eyes met mine, "it's time to get creative and put my craft-loving background to work." I picked up a couple packages of toddler-size disposable diapers at the store and got busy with scissors and duct tape, attempting to fashion a doggy diaper with a hole cut out for Sadie's tail that would be comfortable and provide her enough "wag" room, even given the limited movement she had in her tail, but was still tight and secure enough to prevent leaks or other accidents.

Sadie was a good sport and never complained or fought me as I sat cross-legged with her on the living room floor, struggling to slide the diaper beneath her lifeless back end and around her legs and tail and then tape the whole thing into position. I actually secretly wished she *would* complain or fight me; I was still desperately looking for signs of that bright, spirited dog I had seen just days before, and not this sad, dead-eyed dog staring back at me, listless and uninterested, as I duct-taped another diaper snugly around her withered hips.

Eventually, after much trial and error, I managed to create a doggy diaper that at least seemed workable, in the short term. Longer term I hoped that Sadie would recover enough rectal tone and bladder control to be able to relieve herself outside, without diapers or human intervention. If she didn't achieve at least that modest goal, it was highly unlikely anyone would be willing to adopt her and make her a member of their forever family.

Those first few days were chaotic, but fortunately, Sparky, Kit Kat, and Miss Kitty welcomed Sadie into the fold or, at least in the cats' case, responded to her sudden presence with utter disinterest, in that superiorly feline way that cats are famous for. Sparky seemed to embrace Sadie, mostly because whatever food from Sadie's special high-protein raw diet she didn't eat, the plus-size Sparky was right there to "help" with clearing the leftovers.

I must admit, there were moments when I caught myself, sitting on the soft black sofa in my elegant living room with a cup of coffee, the bright spring light streaming through the windows as the cats curled up beside me and Sparky and Sadie relaxed at my feet, when it just felt "right." It felt like family; it felt complete, and I could picture us like this forever. But those moments were as brief as they were blissful, the spell invariably broken when suddenly Sadie needed a diaper change (again!) or needed me to take her outside to express her bladder, or it was time once again to do the poultice for her forehead, or I had to struggle for forty-five minutes trying to get the necessary pills and supplements inside of her, or I found myself fighting through my own end-of-day fatigue to pick her up for the seemingly hundredth time and haul her up the stairs to bed.

In those moments I'd be overwhelmed with the relentless *need need need*, the seemingly endless patience, determination, and effort it took just to get Sadie from one day to the next. How long could *I* keep this up? I asked myself. Realistically, how long could I keep going? Had I been foolish and shortsighted in letting my heart overrule my head that day at the shelter when Sadie looked up at me, pleading with those sorrowful eyes?

I had to go back to work on Monday. Who would look after Sadie while I was gone all day? Hiring a full-time dog-sitter was certainly out of the question. And money would soon become an issue, between Sadie's expensive raw-meat diet, the many supplements Dr. Jodie had prescribed, and the boxes and boxes of baby diapers.

Dr. Jodie had also recommended Sadie begin a regimen of swimming, acupuncture, healing massage, essential oil baths, and other therapies that were sure to cost a fortune.

Proudly and fiercely independent, I was never comfortable asking other people for help, but I knew that if I kept Sadie, and that was still a big *IF* in my mind, I would have no choice but to reach out for financial support to keep Sadie afloat. But could I reasonably expect other people, especially total strangers, to see the wisdom and value in trying to rescue and rehabilitate one seriously damaged dog? I had found one person in Dr. Jodie willing to give Sadie a chance, but it would likely take an entire army to keep Sadie alive and thriving. What hope did I have of making *that* happen, I wondered in despair.

My biggest supporter, confidante, and shoulder-to-cry-on in those first dark Sadie days was my older sister, Marnette, a college administrator living in South Carolina. I had called her the night I first brought Sadie home and filled her in on the situation. She knew me better than anyone and understood my deep attachment to animals and my history of rescuing those creatures most in need of love and compassion and care, so she wasn't at all surprised to hear that I had brought home yet another stray, and she encouraged me to do everything I could to help Sadie get back on her feet.

When I spoke to Marnette again a few days later, I confided to her that things were not looking good, and Sadie and I were both struggling to make it through the full seven days I had promised her. I was so exhausted, so demoralized and spent at that point, and Sadie, retreating into herself, had made no progress whatsoever and in fact seemed to be regressing, getting a little worse each day. Euthanasia was increasingly seeming like the only realistic option.

"This is one of the hardest things I've ever done," I admitted to Marnette, not proud of the defeat evident in my own voice. "I'm not sure I can keep this up. It's going to take a twenty-four-seven commitment, and I have to be back to work on Monday. And worse than that, Sadie doesn't seem to be responding at all."

She sighed. "Joal, I believe that Sadie is a special animal, a special creature with gifts that haven't yet fully revealed themselves." Marnette's voice, warm and soothing, immediately put me at ease. "I hear it in your voice when you talk about her. You are becoming attached to Sadie, which is why this is so hard. Don't be afraid to open your heart. Don't be afraid to let Sadie in."

"But what if this doesn't work?" My voice cracked and I swallowed hard, fighting back tears. I absolutely refused to cry. I would weep for one of my own fur babies, of course, but not for Sadie, the dog who still belonged to no one. "And what if Sadie doesn't even *want* this?" I asked in despair. "What if, by trying to help her, I'm actually making her suffering worse?"

"Let Sadie guide you," Marnette encouraged gently. "Let her tell you what she wants and needs. I will stand by you and support you in whatever decision you make. I'm here for you, no matter what. But I know you, Joal. When you set your mind to something, nothing is impossible. Remember Flip and Flop?" She chuckled.

Oh yes, I certainly remembered. When I was about six, our collie, Belle, had a litter of puppies. The two runts of the litter we named "Flip" and "Flop" because one had an ear that "flipped" over and the other had an opposite ear that "flopped." They were just babies and far behind their siblings developmentally when I took them aside and worked with them, one on one, until each was able to sit up and stand on its own. Even at age six, I was already showing the emerging signs of my lifelong "never say die" attitude.

"The Joal who worked with Flip and Flop would give Sadie a few more days," Marnette said confidently.

But my insides were tied up in knots, my mind and heart battling for supremacy as Marnette and I said our good-byes. Why did this have to be so difficult? Why couldn't I just do the reasonable, rational, sensible thing and let Sadie go? How had she already managed, in the span of just a few days, to work herself so completely under my skin and into my heart that I could barely imagine a life without her? And yet, it was almost equally difficult to imagine a life *with* Sadie, long term, considering her need for round-the-clock care.

That afternoon was warm and sunny, so, in lieu of making any final decisions, I instead chose to give the perpetually stinky Miss Sadie a bath, outside near the wooden gazebo, where red-breasted robins and black-masked cardinals assembled their delicate nests, and the still-tender late April grass grew soft and dense and emerald-green, not yet bleached and toughened by the harsh summer sun. *If I do take Sadie to be euthanized tomorrow*, I told myself, allowing that possibility to creep into my consciousness, *it's important that she be clean and shiny and smell nice. It should be obvious to everyone that she has been cared for; she has known true human love.*

I still had, stored in my garage, a little kiddie wading pool from when my grandkids, then ages ten and twelve, were younger, so I took that out and filled it half with cold water from the garden hose and half with pots of hot water heated on the kitchen stove.

Once the pool was ready, I lifted Sadie up from the living room floor and carried her outside, steadying her in my arms as I pushed open the screen door with my elbow and laid her down carefully in the long, lush grass. I let her soak up the warmth of the sun as I removed her diaper, wiped her backside, unbandaged her back paw, and prepared to bathe her. She was such a pitiful, pathetic creature, it almost felt like I was invading her privacy, breeching some sacred space, just by gazing upon her broken body.

"Oh Sadie," I sighed, gently rubbing her tummy, "why did someone have to do this to you?" My heart filled with love as my eyes moved across her withered limbs drawn in close to her body, the open sore scraped onto her back paw, the gouged-out, thumb-shaped wound on her forehead, and her narrow, sunken chest with its thin ribs rising into high relief each time she drew a breath.

"If love alone could make you better, you'd be healed in no time at all," I said sadly. Unfortunately, real life was never so simple or so kind. With a sigh I slid my arms beneath Sadie's shoulders and hindquarters, lifted her up and gently lowered her into the water, submerging her paws, legs, and lower body. As usual she didn't complain, she didn't really react at all except to stare at me vacantly, eyes placid and empty, even as I rubbed baby shampoo between my palms and lathered up her fur, scrubbing away the matted dirt, mud, and dried excrement as the water around her thickened and darkened with debris. As I rinsed her off with a steady stream of water poured from a plastic pitcher, her true, vivid colors began to emerge, burnished by the rays of the late afternoon sun.

For the first time I could see that her black fur wasn't just a dull, flat, dusty black as it had first appeared; her coat was actually a sleek, dazzling ebony with lapis lazuli blue undertones, deep and rich as the ink of ancient manuscripts, while her beige fur, more of a chamois-tan and less prevalent than the black, served to contrast and highlight the black with warm, soft, butterscotch-brown accents on her chest, snout, jaw, legs, and paws, along with two whimsical, roundish eyebrows, slightly off-center and just above her amber-colored eyes, adding quirky humor and depths of expression to her gentle, patient face.

"Sadie, you are truly beautiful," I marveled as I towel-dried her back, tummy, shoulders, and paws and cleaned the gummed-up fur around her ears, taking care not to disturb the pockmarked wound that marred her forehead. "This is the real you. If only everyone could see you like this, with your true beauty shining through."

After thoroughly drying her, I clipped away the most badly tangled and deeply matted sections of fur and then sat her upright in the grass so I could brush her vigorously, stroke after stroke, first her left side and then the right. The dying rays of the sun, shimmering on the horizon, combining with the scent of budding lilacs and daffodils and the steady, easy rhythm of the brushstrokes lulled me into a reverie where I felt my soul tiptoeing closer to Sadie, to a wordless place where we could reach each other and communicate, one to one.

"I don't believe your earthly journey is finished, Sadie, I just don't," I stubbornly insisted as I brushed her fur into glossy waves. "There is so much more to you than what you've shown thus far. You have a special gift. But for now, I just need you to give me a sign. Please let me know if I'm doing the right thing." I paused and swallowed hard before I continued, voice trembling. "And, if this isn't right and you want to find your peace in a different place, somewhere beyond the Rainbow Bridge, that's okay, too. I promise I'll be strong enough to let you go. No matter what, I'll never forget these past few days with you."

Sadie looked at me, suddenly making eye contact, wagged her tail a difficult inch or two, and nestled her chin into the crook of my elbow, sighing deeply. "Okay then, girl, it will all be all right," I promised as I wrapped my arms around her shoulders, then kissed the top of her head and buried my nose in her fresh, clean-smelling fur.

That night was a rough one, following a day that had been the most exhausting so far, between the feedings, the forty-five-minute sessions to fill her with her medicine and supplements, the countless trips outside to empty her bladder, and the ongoing diaper changes. Now it was nearly midnight and Sadie just wouldn't settle. I let her sleep in a dog bed on the floor beside my bed, so I'd be close in case she needed anything. Sparky, Miss Kitty, and Kit Kat all slept in the bed beside me so there wasn't room for Sadie, too, not to mention I worried that, without the full use of her legs, if Sadie were on the bed and got scared or panicked in the night, she might roll off, further injuring herself.

Sadie had been whining on and off for almost an hour and I was at my wit's end, having no idea how to help her. "Sadie, what's going on?" I asked in exasperation as I lay flat on my back, staring up at the canopy atop my four-poster bed. Sadie kept nipping at her own backside and rolling her upper body back and forth as if struggling to get comfortable. Too frustrated to deal with this any longer, I climbed out of bed and knelt down beside her on the floor.

"What is it, girl?" I asked softly, stroking her head and rubbing behind her ears. Her tail swished and she let out a low, pitiful moan. As she nosed around her own abdomen, nudging and whining, it occurred to me that she might be missing her lost puppies, the ones she'd delivered shortly before she'd been shot. Instantly, my heart ached for her, for the sorrow and loss she struggled to express.

"Sadie, I know you miss your babies. How fiercely you must have loved them." I imagined Sadie had been a natural-born "mom," nursing and snuggling a litter of five or six wiggly little black-and-tan bundles of joy, bathing them with her tongue until their fur shone, nudging them closer together for warmth, lifting them carefully in her mouth, and gently reprimanding them when they misbehaved. Had she even had time to wean them? I wondered. *Or*, I thought darkly, *had she* just *weaned them, and that was why she was marked for execution?* Having dutifully provided the required litter of healthy puppies, perhaps destined for the evil puppy mills, was she then shot because the puppies were ready for sale and hence Sadie was no longer considered "useful"? At roughly four years old, Sadie might have birthed multiple litters in her lifetime. Perhaps all her babies had been taken away from her, one by one by one.

"Sadie, I wish I could tell you that all your babies are okay, that they have all gone to good homes where they are loved and cherished and cared for." As a mom myself, I understood that a mother's love, the maternal instinct, is one of the most primal and most powerful forces on earth. My two daughters meant everything to me; I would gladly lay down my life for them. I could only imagine the fear, loss, and loneliness that Sadie must be feeling, having her babies cruelly snatched away from her.

Sadie seemed to relax a bit, lowering her guard and responding to my soft words and gentle petting. "Sadie, you are broken, you are wounded, in so many more ways than just those that we can see with our eyes," I told her. "You deserve so much better than what humans have shown you so far." For the first time it occurred to me that maybe it was Sadie's heart, even more so than her body, that truly needed healing.

Sobered by this realization, I helped Sadie settle, then covered her with a blanket and climbed back into bed. I was just starting to nod off when I heard Sadie grab the blanket between her teeth, shake it, then toss it to the side. I knew she'd get cold later on, so I got out of bed and recovered her with the blanket, tucking it around her body on top of the dog bed to keep her warm and protected. No sooner had I gotten myself back into bed and settled than she did it again, wrestling away the blanket and whisking it off to the side.

"Sadie," I said through gritted teeth as I went to cover her yet again, "this is getting *really* annoying." This continued a couple of times, until suddenly it occurred to me: "Sadie is . . . she's playing a game! And she wants me to play with her! Could it be that Sadie has . . . a sense of humor?"

Sure enough, as soon as I agreed to "play" with her, the rules of the game became clear. She wanted me to cover her, then she would toss the blanket off herself, and then it was my turn to cover her again. Her tail wagged more dramatically than I had ever seen it wag before as we played the game, and soon Sparky, Kit Kat, and Miss Kitty were joining in, pulling the blanket, crawling beneath it, snagging it with their paws, and battling not to miss out on all the fun. I laughed until tears, happy tears, streamed down my face. I was amazed to realize that the first time I cried for Sadie, my tears rose not from sorrow but from joy.

I paused to catch my breath. "Sadie, you *are* inside there somewhere, even if I can't always see you, or if your spirit isn't always on show. Any dog with this much personality is nowhere near ready to be put down."

Still on the floor I crossed my legs and cupped Sadie's chin in my hand, peering steadily into her eyes. "Sadie, I know that you understand me, and I believe that you want to get better and walk again. To be honest, I think we have a really rough road ahead of us. I can't make any long-term promises. But let's give it another month, okay? Forget the seven days—let's see what we can accomplish, together, by the end of May. What do you think about that, girl?"

She wagged her tail and panted, and I swear she had a mischievous glint in her eye as she grabbed the blanket between her teeth once more and whisked it triumphantly over her shoulders with a low, teasing growl, followed by a sigh that sounded suspiciously like satisfaction, as all five of us settled in for what would prove to be our first decent night's sleep in several days.

I had no idea what the next month would bring—after all, this was still a dog with overwhelming special needs—but I closed my eyes feeling confident, and fully committed to giving Sadie the best "second chance" on the planet.

CHAPTER THREE
Project Saving Sadie

Trampoline exercises *(photo courtesy Valerie Alba)*.

Whe I woke the next morning, my heart was pounding and my mind racing as I bubbled over with excitement, optimism, and big, ambitious plans for getting Sadie walking again. *We can do this! Hope, faith, and determination can make this happen!* My first cup of coffee was still full to the brim and steaming with a luscious hazelnut aroma as I parked myself at the kitchen table, notepad and pen in hand. Although not yet seven a.m., Sadie had already had her breakfast, her medicine and supplements, her first outdoor bathroom break of the day, and treatment on her forehead and back paw. She was swaddled in a fresh diaper, tail poking through, and curled up at my feet, chin resting contentedly on her front paws. "Okay, girl, if we're going to do this, we're going to do it right. We've got a month to get you walking again, and it's going to take a one-hundred-percent commitment on both our parts to make this happen."

Sadie looked up at me and cocked her head quizzically. I took that as a sign of agreement. Or else it meant she thought I was crazy (which I probably was). I couldn't be sure, so I assumed the best. I scribbled a quick list of all the things I would need to do as I dove headfirst into "Project Saving Sadie":

Call Marnette!!

Call shelter

*Follow-up appt./Arrange Sadie treatments and
therapies w/Dr. Jodie*

Dog-sitter while at work

Contact Think Pawsitive re: swimming

Enlist help of friends and family

*Set up website, Facebook page, social media to share
Sadie news?*

Sadie savings/checking account at bank or credit union

*Arrange meet-and-greets with Sadie for potential
donors/supporters?*

Hmmm. Some quick figuring showed that it would likely
take somewhere in the region of three thousand dollars a
month to pay for Sadie's medicine, supplements, treatments, therapy, and other care. Three thousand dollars! My
spirits tumbled and the optimism with which I had begun
the day immediately evaporated. It was one thing to have
the will to help Sadie, but it was a very different thing to
have, or to find, the resources to actually make it happen.
How in the world would I come up with three thousand
dollars a month, month in and month out, for as long as it
took to get Sadie fully rehabilitated?

I had been enjoying a successful career as a transitional
organization specialist for several years, but like many independent contractors and small business owners, the combi-
nation of an unpredictable work schedule, taxes, expenses,
and lack of benefits meant there wasn't much left over at
the end of the month, and certainly not three thousand
dollars.

I was prepared to ask family and friends for help, but realistically there would be a limit to how much, and how frequently, they would be willing to contribute. For this utterly crazy plan to work, I would need to solicit funds from total strangers, a thought that made me deeply uncomfortable.

But one look at Sadie curled up at my feet reminded me that I wouldn't be asking for myself, I was asking on behalf of Sadie. Maybe if I framed the message by saying, "I've found this poor dog and here's how we're trying to help her," that would make the need more real and more concrete for people and they would be inspired to contribute. I believe that people are generally good-hearted and want to help; often they just don't know what to do. Maybe, if people were touched by Sadie's story, they would offer support. But three thousand dollars a month worth of support? That thought was overwhelming. But I had to at least give it a try. I reached down and stroked Sadie's head. When she looked up at me with her kind, patient, trusting eyes and feebly wagged her tail, I felt confident that any efforts on her behalf would be worth it.

I put on my best "happy voice" as I phoned Marnette and told her that I had come to a decision and was going to give Sadie another month to show some serious improvement. "Oh Joal, that's wonderful!" she exclaimed when I shared the news. "If anyone can make this work, you can."

"But it's going to cost a fortune," I added quickly, hoping not to dampen her mood. "Maybe three thousand dollars a month. I don't know where I'll come up with that kind of money."

"Don't worry—I'll do everything I can to help," she promised. "I already have a few people in mind who can help us raise funds online. I will reach out to them, and everyone else I can possibly think of. When people hear Sadie's story, they will want to help."

I deeply appreciated Marnette's support, knowing that she had a full-time job and other commitments and lived hundreds of miles away, and yet I felt confident she would be our best partner and resource, always going the extra mile. I realized with a start that Marnette was falling in love with Sadie, even though they had yet to meet in person. I was reminded again of how blessed I was to have such a sister.

"Okay, so we've got Dr. Jodie and we've got Marnette," I told Sadie. "That's a start. The first two official members of Team Sadie are firmly on board."

After speaking to Marnette, my next call was to the shelter in Kenosha, letting them know that I was ready to begin the paperwork to make Sadie's adoption official—not after one week or one month, but immediately. In my mind, I was not yet Sadie's "forever" mom, and I was still keeping a part of my heart separate and unreachable, not willing to endure the potential heartbreak of letting myself fall in love. There was still a real possibility that if we weren't able to rehab Sadie and get her walking again, the kindest thing would be to have her euthanized.

I had made a promise, both to her and to myself, that Sadie would never go back to a shelter to live out the rest of her days in a drafty basement, locked in a cold metal cage, incontinent and unable to walk; scared, lonely, and bereft of human love. Either this plan would work, or I would make the compassionate choice to let Sadie go and find her freedom beyond the Rainbow Bridge. And the only way I'd be free to make that agonizing decision was by first making Sadie's adoption official, so I would have the final say over those tough choices.

I took Sadie for her first follow-up appointment with Dr. Jodie that afternoon. Dr. Jodie didn't seem at all surprised that I had decided to give Sadie at least another month; I think she had known right away that I was developing a bond with this very special dog. Dr. Jodie's exam revealed that Sadie was already showing signs of improvement as a result of my attention and tender loving care. The poultice I was using on her forehead was drawing the bullet closer to the surface, and the salve and bandages were helping heal the sore on her back foot.

But now that I had committed one hundred percent to rehabbing Sadie and getting her walking again, we needed to kick Sadie's treatment plan into the highest possible gear, and we needed to start immediately. Dr. Jodie proposed we spend the next two months building up Sadie's strength and overall health by continuing her high-protein, nutrient-rich diet, supplements, and exercise, and by adding swimming, massage, and intense physical therapy, so that by July she would be strong enough to handle surgery to amputate her left back leg, thus allowing her to walk on the three remaining good legs, once fully strengthened.

I was candid with Dr. Jodie about my financial situation, so we struck a deal in which I would drop Sadie off at Dr. Jodie's clinic at nine every morning before I went to work and then pick her up again after work at five p.m. While Sadie was at Dr. Jodie's during the day, the staff would work with her whenever they had a free moment between patients, performing acupuncture (in hopes of stimulating and regenerating her damaged, weakened nerves), deep muscle massages, and essential oil baths.

I also arranged for Sadie to go swimming three times a week at "Think Pawsitive," a nearby dog training and agility center that included a specially designed indoor heated swimming pool for dogs. In addition, I committed to working with Sadie myself, one-on-one, for several hours a day, before and after work, on exercises designed to stimulate her mind and strengthen her back and her good legs, along with the rest of her body. This would all prove to be as exhausting as it sounds, but when I'm "all in," I'm "all in," and Sadie needed to be my top priority if this was going to work.

My next step was setting up a "Saving Sadie" bank account at the nearby Landmark Credit Union, so people, if interested, would be able to contribute to the cost of Sadie's ongoing care. I wasn't sure if anyone would give anything, to be honest, but I had to remain hopeful and optimistic, for Sadie's sake.

Once the credit union account was up and running, it was time to start reaching out to family and friends for support. I knew we'd need more help than they alone could provide, but it was the obvious place to start, especially for the immediate bills, which were already beginning to pile up. Swallowing my natural reluctance and discomfort about asking people for money, I drafted an informational flyer that I could email to family and friends. At the top was a cute picture of Sadie, stretched out in the grass with a bright yellow bandanna knotted jauntily around her neck. Below that I wrote: "Will You Please Help Me??" And then the body of the message:

Dear Family and Friends,

In life we have many choices. Each given moment we can choose to do right or wrong, say yes or no, or to take or give. I was moved to make a choice based on being chosen by the look of a dog in need. I just had to help when no one else was choosing to help. I invite you to join me in making a choice, a choice to help with unconditional love and support. With your help we will make a difference in the life of an innocent victim.

A week ago I was on autopilot, doing work for a client. We chose to donate discarded blankets and linens to a no-kill animal shelter in southeastern Wisconsin . . .

The flyer went on to describe how I found and rescued Sadie, and how she needed acupuncture and swim therapy, in addition to other treatment, in preparation for her surgery. I ended by sharing our goal to give Sadie a quality of life as close to normal as possible and asking people to contribute whatever they could, whether five dollars or five hundred dollars.

At the bottom of the page I included three more photos of Sadie, one showing me bandaging the sore on her foot, one helping her relieve herself, and one of me dabbing ointment on her forehead wound. I chose those photos because they demonstrated in a concrete and visual way how Sadie required intensive, hands-on care, but also highlighted her intelligent face and beautiful black-and-tan markings. "You are such a lovely girl," I reassured her, cupping her chin in my hands and massaging the base of her ears with my thumbs. She closed her eyes and sighed with pleasure. "Let's hope these pictures touch other people's hearts as much as you've touched mine."

With help from some of my more tech-savvy friends, I imported my list of email contacts, composed a brief cover letter, attached the flyer and hit Send to over two hundred of my family, friends, and others, feeling a mixture of hope, anxiety, and trepidation. I am not by nature a deeply religious person, but looking back now, I can see that one of the many ways that Sadie changed me was by teaching me the true meaning of faith and what it means to believe in something wholeheartedly; how to have hope when having hope is your only option. "Okay, Sadie," I told her, "it's out of our hands now. Let's cross our fingers and paws and pray that some magic happens."

In the midst of so much frenetic activity, between the hours of at-home therapy, swimming three times a week, long days at the vet, diapering, wound care, email and Internet campaigns, and struggles to raise money, Sadie had her first real breakthrough on May 3, only nine days after I first brought her home, when she took her first few wobbly "bunny hops" toward the car as we were getting ready to go to Dr. Jodie's.

In order to encourage Sadie to relearn how to urinate outside on her own, I would remove her diaper and let her spend some time playing in the grass. It always broke my heart to see her struggling so, raising herself up on her front legs and trying to make her scrawny, spindly back legs straighten and support her weight. She looked so helpless, so damaged and disabled in those moments. But I knew it was good for her; good to get the fresh air, the exercise, and the opportunity to remember how it felt to relieve herself in the grass, doggy-style, just like she used to do before she was shot.

But on this day, rather than just rolling around and staggering forward, trying to drag her lower body, she hopped! She actually made a concentrated, coordinated movement, pushing up and forward on her front legs while simultaneously pulling her back legs up and over. She looked surprised at her own progress, then immediately did it again, taking another wobbly bunny hop. Then a third hop and a fourth. She paused to catch her breath, panting hard. My heart soared and my eyes filled with tears.

"That's my girl!" I exclaimed. "Sadie, this just goes to show that you *do* want to walk again. And it shows how determined you are to make it happen!" It also illustrated the incredible progress she had made in just nine days. "First-day Sadie" would never have had the strength, energy, or desire to propel herself forward by hopping.

Sadie took a total of twenty hops that day. She looked utterly exhausted as I picked her up and carried her the last few steps to the car, holding her close and kissing her head as her heart beat wildly against her ribs and she struggled to catch her breath. "That's my good girl," I soothed her, whispering in her velvety ear. "Keep this up and you'll be back to your old self in no time."

After our appointment with Dr. Jodie, I couldn't wait to call Marnette and tell her about Sadie's progress. She was as excited as I was to hear the great news, but my mood quickly turned bittersweet as I hung up the phone. I had no one else with whom I could share this major milestone.

When I had told Jami-Lyn I was keeping Sadie for another month, she expressed skepticism. I knew her concern sprang only from love, and her fear that I would lavish so much time, money, energy, and attention on a dog that might still have to be euthanized in the end. As a daughter and as a vet, she felt it was her mission to protect me.

My other daughter, Joey, seemed to agree with Jami-Lyn. She especially didn't want my grandchildren, twelve-year-old Miranda and ten-year-old Connor, to meet Sadie yet, for fear they would become attached to a dog that was not long for this world.

Deep down I knew my girls might well be right. A few wobbly hops were a long, long way from walking, and there was no guarantee that Sadie would ever achieve that goal. Was I being foolish for getting my hopes up? *No*, I told myself sternly. *Don't start thinking that way. Negativity will get you nowhere. Focus on Sadie. You* can *make her better.*

By the middle of May, Project Saving Sadie had reached a fever pitch, even though we were still only two weeks in. Our first Saving Sadie website and Facebook fan page, both created and maintained by Marnette, were up and running and, most important, looked terrific. Now we were able to accept donations via credit card through Sadie's website, in addition to the checks being sent to Landmark Credit Union.

Marnette was absolutely amazing during this period, as expected. She was working every spare moment that she had

to post any new content and updates about Sadie on the website. Meanwhile I was running her ragged, constantly sending
her more photos and information to post. We always asked
people to pass on Sadie's website address to others so that
we could increase awareness and hopefully increase funding. I believe that the message that Marnette was sending
out to people was so effective because it was so essentially
simple, consisting of three heartfelt requests: she asked
people to pray for Sadie, to contribute funds, and to spread
the message about helping Sadie.

Marnette had also started a ChipIn account online to
raise money for Sadie's upkeep and care. The company is no
longer in business today, but at the time ChipIn was an Internet crowdfunding platform similar to GoFundMe that allowed people to follow a specific fund-raising campaign
and then donate money directly through a link on the
ChipIn page. Marnette had spread the word widely to her
friends and contacts, and small amounts of money had already been contributed. We set a goal of raising eight thousand dollars in two months, to pay for Sadie's upcoming
surgery.

Marnette had also gotten in touch with a woman named
Laura Simpson, the founder of the Harmony Fund and the
Great Animal Rescue Chase, two charities based in Holden,
Massachusetts. Devoted to helping "last chance" animals
and the organizations that support them, Laura maintained
websites that reached over sixty thousand visitors each
month and that served as a tremendous resource for people
wishing to help animals. Laura, even though she didn't
know us, was instrumental in getting the funding ball
rolling for Sadie after she featured Sadie's story on her site.

As soon as the first story posted, emails of encouragement, along with small donations, started rolling in.

As more and more people heard about Sadie's plight, there was some funding available to help supplement the money that I was paying out of pocket for Sadie's care. Marnette literally worked every waking moment, before and after her full-time job, to help get the word out about Sadie, and the response was incredible. Soon we had people all around the world praying for Sadie and sending her cards and good wishes.

Sometimes during these early weeks I found myself looking at Sadie in amazement. Here she was, often cowering in a corner, a traumatized, underweight, unassuming black-and-tan dog, still not able to walk, not really able to do much of anything, and still prone to moments of vacantness, listlessness, and extreme passivity, and yet people cared about her. People responded to her story, even people who lived hundreds or thousands of miles away and had never met her and probably never would. Even so, they were touched enough by Sadie's story to send a note or an email, or make a five-dollar donation toward her care. I was truly humbled by the impact Sadie was having every day, even though at that point I could never have imagined what Sadie's future held, or what her extraordinary gift to the world would ultimately be.

But even with the wonderfully positive response to our email campaign and Internet outreach efforts, I knew deep down that it wasn't going to be enough. We needed to widen our base, spread our message much further, and reach far more people if we had any hope of keeping Sadie afloat. Paying for advertising was definitely out of the question given our shoestring budget, so our only hope was to try to get the media interested in covering Sadie's story. I had no background in journalism or public relations but I did have experience in sales, so that's how I approached the task: I needed to "sell" the media on the merits of doing a story about Sadie.

Similar to the email announcements I had sent out to family and friends, I created an email "pitch" about Sadie and sent it to dozens and dozens of our local media in southeastern Wisconsin. This was a long, tedious, frustrating process, and most of my emails were ignored, or answered with a polite decline.

Finally, we got our first "nibble" when the *Waukesha Freeman*, a large local suburban daily newspaper, responded to my pitch. They sent Dave Fidlin, a freelance writer and reporter, along with photographer Charles Auer, to the house to interview and photograph Sadie and me.

My excitement about the interview was tempered by a mild case of nerves, wanting to present both Sadie and myself in the most positive light. It wasn't enough for Dave to fall in love with Sadie; Dave's readers needed to fall in love with her as well.

It turned out I needn't have worried—Sadie hit it off right away with Dave, a fresh-faced young man with a crisp buzz cut and a broad, boyish grin. He listened with interest and took copious notes as I described how I stumbled across Sadie at the shelter and how she had already changed my life in just a few short weeks. I emphasized how much progress Sadie had made so far, and what a difference support from others was making.

Sadie was a good sport throughout, posing for photos outside in the grass, but of course we couldn't know for certain how the interview had gone until Tuesday, May 15, 2012, the day the article appeared in print. As soon as I found out that the story was running in that day's edition, I hopped in my SUV and drove a few blocks to the nearest gas station, rushed inside, and grabbed the first copy off the pile of newspapers arranged in a haphazard stack alongside the display racks of beef jerky, bubble gum, and chewing tobacco.

I gave a little shriek of joy as my eye jumped directly to the paper's masthead, where a teaser boldly announced: *Help give Sadie a second chance—Muskego woman determined to help dog who was shot twice in horrific act of cruelty.* Beside the teaser was a full-color close-up photo of Sadie.

"Oh yes!" I bellowed, then glanced up to see the confused expression on the face of the young man behind the counter. "This is my dog," I announced proudly, pointing to the headline and photo. *Yes,* I thought suddenly, *Sadie is my dog now. She belongs to me. I may not be her "forever" mom yet, but she will never again belong to anyone else.*

My heart was pumping hard as I turned to page 4A, the beginning of the Local section, and there was Sadie's photo again, even bigger this time and in black and white, beside the headline: A SECOND CHANCE FOR SADIE—MUSKEGO WOMAN DETERMINED TO HELP DOG.

> MUSKEGO—It started out as a routine day for Joal Derse Dauer. Pillows and blankets in hand, the Muskego resident planned to donate the

items to a local no-kill animal shelter, an act
she does routinely . . .

I was thrilled as I skimmed the rest of the article, which
took up most of the page. I bought several copies of the
paper and took them home, where I sat at my kitchen table
and read and re-read the article again and again. The story
was clear, concise, and focused, emphasizing the progress
Sadie had already made and including details about how to
contribute to the Saving Sadie fund, either online or through
the credit union.

"Sadie, we are doing it! We are really doing it, girl, and we
are on our way!" She looked up at me and cocked her head
to one side in that quickly-becoming-her-trademark, "my
mom must be crazy" way. I knelt down on the kitchen floor
beside her, wrapped my arms around her shoulders, and
gave her a huge kiss atop her glossy black head. "You are a
star. Just keep doing what you're doing, Sadie, and soon
everyone will be inspired to help."

And then I did something I probably shouldn't have
done—I went to my study, logged on to my computer, and
checked our Saving Sadie ChipIn account. My heart fell.
After a busy couple of days, donations had trickled to almost nothing. We were so far short of our goal. For the first
time a terrible reality shook me to the core. *Sadie wants to
live. And she wants to walk again; she has made that very
clear. I am willing to do anything and everything I can to
help her. But in the end there just might not be enough
money to make that happen. If I can't raise enough
funds, I will have no choice but to have Sadie euthanized.*

She's never going back to the shelter, and I can't support her on my own.

Suddenly I felt a slight pressure against my calf. I looked down. Somehow Sadie had managed to pull herself from the kitchen into my study and was leaning against my leg, in solidarity and support. "Oh Sadie," I sighed, reaching down to stroke her head and rub behind her ears. "I know what you would tell me if you could speak: *Have faith. Be strong. Stay the course. Please don't give up on me, Mom. You promised me a second chance. I believe in you. Don't give up on me now.*"

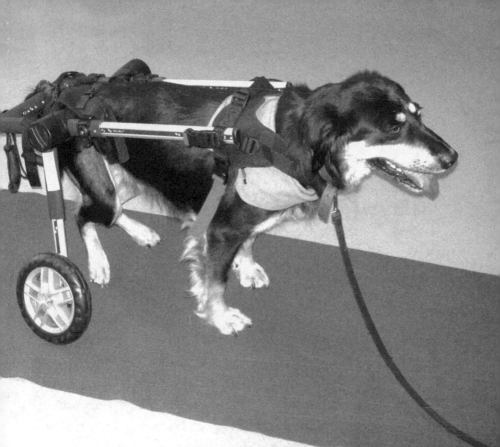

CHAPTER FOUR

Who's Rehabbing
Whom?

What is it about dogs that allows them to touch our souls so deeply? Denied the gift of human speech and comprehension, what magic happens, what potent alchemy spins out from their soft paws, wagging tails, and lolling tongues, from their cold, damp noses and warm doggy breath? What hidden channels, what secret languages of exchange allow messages to pass, wordlessly yet powerfully, from their hearts to ours and back again? What habits, gestures, and expressions allow us to know each other better than we know ourselves? Dogs believe in us; by accepting our love, they grant us the wings to become our better angels and rise above our lesser selves.

Where Sadie was concerned, I may have been determined to remain a skittish, skeptical lover, a headstrong Jane Austen heroine unwilling to relinquish my whole heart to her for fear of having it smashed into a million pieces, but already, even in that first month after bringing Sadie home, I could feel myself changing, responding to the powerful influence she was having on my life.

The ongoing demands of Sadie's care were pushing me beyond my comfort zone in so many ways. I had always been a social person, comfortable both in groups and engaging one-on-one, but now I had to be proactively social, constantly reaching out to solicit media coverage and financial support for Sadie. I had to learn never to take no for an answer because Sadie's future, her very life, in fact, depended on it. I had to be more organized, more focused, more patient, and more committed than ever before. I learned to open up, and to be more forgiving, of myself and of Sadie, especially when she was nowhere close to walking yet and still wasn't able, even with all the physical therapy and exercises and supplements and treatments, to do many of the things I expected her to be doing by now, now as the lilac-and-baby's-breath freshness of early May was ripening, marching toward June and the blazing promise of a glorious Midwestern summer.

By nature a perfectionist, I was learning to lower my expectations and to savor and celebrate victories, no matter how small. Fortunately, Sadie was achieving some meaningful milestones even as she failed to clear the highest hurdles I'd set out for her. For example, she was occasionally urinating on her own, although she still needed a diaper to handle leaks and prevent accidents between bathroom breaks. Even better, she was now defecating, or what I prefer to call "detoxing," on her own. Dr. Jodie had been right that the special diet she had prescribed had softened her stools and allowed Sadie to regain control over this important function.

To be honest, Sadie would have probably started detoxing on her own much sooner, if I had only realized that my Sadie was by nature a modest girl and, like most people, desired some privacy when she "did her business." She would hop/crawl as far away from me as possible and then hide when she wanted to go. Once I understood that, I always gave Sadie her space when requested and tried not to hover like an overanxious helicopter mom!

By week three, Sadie had gone into heat, which surprised me, but was also reassuring because it suggested that internally her body was responding to the diet and supplements, becoming stronger and more stable as she recovered from the trauma of her injuries and the subsequent lack of nutrition and proper care that she had endured before I found her. "You're getting better, girl; you're making progress every single day," I would whisper in her ear during those close, quiet, intimate moments when the day's insanity had subsided and it was just the two of us, as I washed her backside or changed her diaper or prepared the poultice for her head. It had been years—decades, in fact—since my children were babies and I had had a living creature depend on me so completely, looking to me to provide warmth, protection, shelter, cleanliness, and nourishment. I was Sadie's lifeline to the world and her only chance for survival. It was both sobering and inspiring when I dried Sadie off after a bath, rubbing and fluffing her damp, dark fur in a big old beach towel, and she would just stare placidly into my face, her deep amber eyes helpless with grace, gratitude, and love.

Meanwhile, the ambitious Saving Sadie project that Marnette and I had initiated continued in earnest. Day and night, it seemed like all we were doing was working on and marketing Sadie; eating, breathing, sleeping Sadie. We looked at every contact as a challenge and an adventure, and we just kept on trying to reach more and more people, raising money and awareness. Marnette's contact Laura

Simpson kept Sadie in the spotlight, constantly posting new articles on her websites and also on the CARE2.com website, which helped tremendously, bringing in donations and forging relationships that we never could have made happen on our own.

All this chaos was exciting, and nerve-racking, but I also sometimes worried that the rest of my life was slipping away from me. I was exhausted at work, rarely saw my friends, and found it difficult to talk to my daughters, who worried about what adopting Sadie was doing to me. I missed my girls so much, my heart aching in a way only a mother can truly understand. I couldn't imagine having to choose between my daughters or my dog—I just prayed it never reached that point.

If only Jami-Lyn and Joey would spend some time with Sadie, I thought ruefully, *they could see how much progress she is making, and they would understand why this is so important to me.* But in the meantime, waiting for them to come around became yet another type of hope with which I was learning to live, negotiating those fractious personal and familial curves, those rough and bumpy places where want and need, conflict and desire overlapped and intersected.

As the weeks went on, I remained fully committed to getting Sadie walking again, but from a practical standpoint, it was becoming really difficult to carry her everywhere, or to ask her to "bunny hop" any farther than a few feet at a time. She was growing stronger, gaining muscle every day, and was now inching toward a healthy fifty-plus pounds. But meanwhile my poor arms struggled to keep up with her increasing size and weight. So I decided to buy her a wagon. "It will just be temporary," I promised myself, "so it will be easier to transport her when we aren't in the car."

Money was tight, so I went on Craigslist and bought a used child's wagon, a modular, red, hard plastic "Little Tikes" model with a long stiff handle for pulling. As soon as I picked it up I realized how large and unwieldy it would be, especially getting it into and out of my SUV, but there was no way to return it. My friend Skip McCabe of Mundelein, Illinois, was generous enough to paint the wagon in Sadie's signature colors of yellow and green. I hoped we wouldn't need the wagon for too long; only until Sadie was ready to have her back leg amputated so she could walk again.

Around this time, I received a phone call from a woman named Joanie, offering to give us the "Walkin' Wheels" that her disabled dog wasn't using. You've probably seen dogs with this type of apparatus, which is basically a wheelchair for dogs, with two wheels at the back legs and attached to the torso with metal bars along either side and straps around the chest and hindquarters. Joanie, whose dog was a patient of Dr. Jodie's, had heard about Sadie at Dr. Jodie's clinic, where as part of our marketing efforts we had put up a poster with pictures of Sadie and our website info, along with a jar to collect donations toward her care.

"My dog just never adjusted to the Walkin' Wheels," Joanie explained over the phone. "So if you are interested, I'd be happy to let you have it. I can drop it off at the clinic." Her offer was very generous—I knew from my own research that these devices were very expensive. And yet I couldn't accept—I just couldn't bring myself to consider the possibility that Sadie might never walk again unaided.

"Thank you so much for the offer, but Sadie will be walking again soon," I explained. "At the moment I'm transporting her in a kid's wagon, but we shouldn't need that for much longer."

"All right," she replied. "That's great news." She paused, then continued, sounding hesitant. "But if you change your mind, just give me a call. The offer still stands."

I hung up the phone and looked at Sadie, curled up contentedly on the kitchen floor near my feet. "You will be walking again soon, won't you, girl?" I asked tentatively. She raised her head and gazed up at me, but otherwise didn't respond.

Toward the end of May, Dr. Jodie said she believed Sadie was now strong enough to undergo surgery to remove the bullet from her forehead. I had been scrupulous about mixing the powder and liquid and applying the thick poultice twice a day, and while it had drawn the bullet closer to the surface, clearly, it was never going to come out on its own.

"Couldn't we just leave the bullet in there?" I asked, taken aback by the suggestion. "It doesn't seem to be bothering Sadie at all."

"We could," Dr. Jodie agreed as we sat cross-legged on the floor in her cozy treatment room, with Sadie stretched out between us, rows of acupuncture needles neatly aligned along her torso and legs. Plump, overstuffed pillows supported our backs as soft music played in the background.

"But on the other hand, we don't know if the bullet is

causing her any pain or headaches or other discomfort. There's also the chance it could be releasing heavy metals or other toxins into her bloodstream. I think we should take it out. It's a relatively minor surgery," she added quickly, no doubt reading the concern on my face. "We wouldn't even need to keep her overnight." Before I could reply, she continued, "I think we should remove the cyst on her tail at the same time. It seems to be getting bigger, so it really should come out, too."

I paused a moment to catch my breath. A two-part surgery? Was Sadie strong enough for that? She'd been through so much in her life, especially in recent months, what if an operation, even a minor one, was more than her poor, brutalized body could tolerate? I worried that she might still be compromised in ways we weren't even aware of. Even so, I trusted Dr. Jodie, and I knew she always had Sadie's best interest at heart. This was a Tuesday, so we scheduled the surgery for the following Monday, June 4, allowing Sadie a few more days to rehab and recover before the operation.

When we returned home from the appointment, Sadie's surgery was weighing heavily on my mind, as was the fact that it was now the 29th of May, which meant there were only two days left in the "one month" I had given Sadie to show significant improvement before deciding whether to continue with her rehab. She had made some progress, without a doubt, but yet if I were to be brutally honest, she was nowhere near where I hoped and believed she would be by now. The strength and feeling in her back legs was minimal, even after all the swimming, exercises, and acupuncture to stimulate and regenerate her nerves. We were struggling to get media coverage for Sadie's story, and funds were running desperately low.

Feeling despondent, I phoned Marnette. I told her about scheduling Sadie's surgery for Monday and my despair over Sadie's lack of progress at this all-important "one-month" milestone.

"Have you checked the ChipIn page recently?" Marnette asked.

"No," I admitted. "I've just been too busy, and too exhausted, to check it out."

"Take a look. You might be surprised." Her tone of voice was warm, and in my mind's eye I pictured her twinkly smile.

"You mean right now?" I asked.

"Yes. Are you near your computer?"

"I can be."

I took the phone into my study, turned on the computer, logged in, and then opened our ChipIn page. My heart immediately tumbled to my feet. We had only managed to raise $1,165 towards our goal of $8,000, and we were almost halfway through the funding period. *And Marnette wants me to be* happy *about this?*

"Marnette, we haven't even raised twelve hundred dollars yet, and it's almost the first of June," I said glumly. "And we've been working so hard on this, too. I know how much time, energy, and effort you've been putting into Saving Sadie."

"Joal, I'm not talking about the fund-raising."

"You aren't? Then why did you want me to check the ChipIn page?"

"Read the messages."

"Messages? What messages?"

"The messages and comments people posted when they made their donations." She sighed, sounding exasperated. "Joal, you need to look beyond just the money, the dollars and cents, in order to see the complete picture, the full impact that Sadie is having on people."

"Okay. Let's see." I quickly scrolled down the page and began reading:

Wishing you and Sadie all the very best as you work towards a recovery for her. BC, Canada.
—Senara M.

God bless you for taking such wonderful care of Sadie. I truly believe the Dog is God's most beautiful creation. You will never find another human loves you as much as your dog.
—Thomas C.

Just lost my Border collie called Sadie aged 18. Miss her so much. Hope this contribution helps for your Sadie. God bless her. xxxx
—Sandra Q.

Sending my prayers and blessings to you, Sadie.
—Robert R.

God Bless You and Sadie, too.
—Cynthia G.

"Well, what do you think?" Marnette asked as I continued skimming the page. In truth I was speechless. The donations people were making were small—five or ten dollars, in most cases—but the comments were so touching and heartfelt, they were worth a million dollars each.

"I'm really humbled," I admitted, feeling sheepish. "I was so focused on the money, on reaching our goal and monitoring the bottom line, that I didn't even notice the comments."

"That's part of Sadie's gift to you," Marnette explained. "To make you notice the little things in life and help you focus on what truly matters."

Marnette was right—here was Sadie, working her magic on me yet again, and me not even realizing it. Not for the first time I wondered, who was saving whom? Was I rehabbing Sadie, or was she in fact rehabbing me?

Along with our Internet and email outreach efforts and approaches to the media, I worked on arranging a series of meet-and-greets for Sadie, to introduce her to the community and show people in a really concrete and visual way how their donations were helping her recover. Sadie's first public appearance was Friday, June 1, 2012, at "Jammin' on Janesville" here in Muskego.

I put a lot of effort into getting Sadie ready, washing her, grooming her, brushing her, tying a colorful bandanna around her neck and making sure she looked "perfect." I wanted everyone to see how beautiful and wonderful she was and then, hopefully, be inspired to offer help.

But I worried, too—how would Sadie react to the crowds, the noise, and so many strange new people all at once? I envisioned a nightmare full of eager children with busy hands; fireworks and sparklers and Roman candles;

cars backfiring, and other dogs on leashes with their curious, inquisitive noses wanting to smell and engage and explore.

I had no idea what Sadie's life in Kentucky had been like,
but if she had been a breeder for puppy mills, she probably
hadn't spent much if any time being socialized to people,
and certainly she had had limited contact with anyone
other than the shelter staff, myself, and Dr. Jodie and her
staff since she'd been shot. So I naturally worried about
how Sadie would react to this new, and potentially upset-
ting, experience.

Still, I knew we had to give it a try, for Sadie's sake, so I
put my reservations on hold as I loaded Sadie into her
brand-new (at least to us) Little Tikes plastic wagon and we
made our way to Jammin' on Janesville, and to our station at
the booth outside Dr. Jodie's clinic, the Animal Doctor Holistic Veterinary Complex.

How to describe Jammin' on Janesville? Well, imagine a
carnival, street fair, music festival, and good old-fashioned
Midwestern block party, then multiply it by twenty and that
might give you some idea of the scope of the event. It had
originally been founded a year earlier, in 2011, by the
Muskego Chamber of Commerce and Tourism to help keep
local businesses alive and thriving while serious road con-
struction tore up parts of Janesville Road, the main commercial thoroughfare that ran straight through the heart of
Muskego.

The event was set for the first Fridays of June, July, and
August, running from five to nine p.m. All the businesses
along a three-mile stretch of Janesville Road set up tables,

booths, and exhibits in front of their establishments, so the public could come and linger, shop, and learn more about and support local businesses, all while enjoying food, live music, beer and wine tastings, games, raffles, demonstrations, and other entertainment.

As Sadie and I made our way down the street, I was bowled over by the crazy party atmosphere that had descended on our normally sedate little suburb. The street was full of honking, beeping traffic and people on motorcycles and hundreds of pedestrians, moving from tent to tent, table to table, enjoying the warm, hazy, early summer evening. Twangy country-rock bands staged impromptu concerts in parking lots, clowns twisted balloons into hats and swans and sailboats, and vendors hawked jewelry as giddy children played beanbag toss and had their faces painted with bright, colorful designs.

And the food! Nothing says summer in Wisconsin like fairground food: roasted corn on the cob, with its warm, rich, caramel-y aroma, papery husks singed and seared and then peeled before being plunged into huge open vats of velvety, melted golden butter and doused with salt and pepper and spicy Cajun seasoning. My mouth watered as we passed the funnel cakes, cotton candy, saltwater taffy, and the sizzling double- and triple-level grills cooking succulent burgers, bratwurst, kielbasa, and Italian sausage.

Rather than being intimidated or overwhelmed, Sadie seemed utterly mesmerized by the sights, the sounds, the smells, sitting up straight and tall in her wagon, ears tipped forward, tongue wagging, and eyes alert to everything. When we reached the clinic, Dr. Jodie was outside, preparing her booth in the parking lot. "Well, what do you think?" she asked me, smiling brightly as her loose brown curls bobbed toward her shoulders.

"This is absolutely incredible," I replied, shaking my head in amazement. "It's like everyone in Muskego came out tonight, and also brought along ten of their friends."

I settled Sadie in her wagon in our designated spot next to the stand where Dr. Jodie had vendors selling hot dogs and caramel corn. The clinic would remain open throughout the evening, so visitors could go inside and tour the treatment suites, the emergency room, and the "Kitty Camp" where Dr. Jodie housed a number of unadoptable cats, and also learn more about the essential oils, special diets, and holistic pet care products she sold at the clinic. We had arranged a "safe space" with blankets and low lighting for Sadie in one of the exam rooms in back, so I'd have a quiet, private place to take her if she became overwhelmed by all the activity, but so far Sadie was loving every moment of the festival.

I viewed our presence at Jammin' on Janesville as primarily informational. I didn't feel comfortable asking people for money directly; that seemed degrading to Sadie and felt too much like begging or panhandling to me. Instead I had made up and printed "Saving Sadie" business cards, postcards, and informational flyers to hand out to people who approached us. Every item included our website URL, www.SavingSadie.com, so the hope was that after meeting Sadie in person, people would be interested and inspired enough to go to the website and make a donation via our ChipIn account.

We hadn't been in position in front of the clinic for long

when people, especially families, began migrating toward Sadie, gathering around her wagon, petting her, stroking her head, and asking what had happened to her and why she was in a wagon. I cleared my throat and explained, "Sadie lived in Kentucky, where some very bad people shot her in the head and back after she had puppies."

I wanted to be truthful, but also sensitive about how I phrased things when young people were present. "Because of the bullet in her back, she can't walk like other dogs. Some kind people brought her to Wisconsin and I adopted her. Together she and I are working really hard on exercises and therapy so she can walk again."

Hearing that, some of the teenagers started crying, and I noticed several of the adults were misty-eyed as well as they caressed Sadie or patted her head. Sadie, for her part, was an absolute trouper, showing no fear or shyness or uncertainty, just patience and love as she gracefully, and gratefully, accepted all the affection.

"Please don't feel sad for Sadie," I implored the crowd. "She is a very happy dog and not in any pain. Hers is a story of pure love and second chances." Suddenly a new and striking thought occurred to me, and I was moved to share it with our audience. "Sadie may not be able to walk right now, but everybody has at least one problem or one thing wrong with them. Everyone deserves a second chance. Sadie can teach people all about acceptance, and focusing on what you *can* do, not what you can't."

Suddenly people's tears and frowns transformed into smiles as they moved in closer to Sadie, surrounding her in a loose but powerful circle of love. I handed out Sadie's business card to everyone within reach and was a bit embarrassed when some people started placing money in the empty water dish beside Sadie's wagon as if it were a collection jar. "Please go to our website to follow Sadie's progress," I said, speaking over the electric riffs of the Led Zeppelin cover band warming up a few booths over. "With your help, we will get Sadie walking again."

Sometime later, the crowd thinned a bit as the sky turned to dusk and the air became dense with the smell of charcoal smoke and citronella candles and the angry, metallic buzz of hungry mosquitoes. I lifted Sadie out of her wagon, laid her in the grass, and gave her some water and a few well-deserved treats, which she sniffed, nibbled, and then slowly savored each bite. I sat down beside her and stroked her shoulder, still warm from the sun. "That's my good girl. There are more treats for you at home."

As we sat and relaxed side by side, my mind kept casting back to the faces of all the people, men and women, adults and kids, who'd met Sadie, who'd listened so intently to her story and been so moved by what they'd heard. What I'd suspected from the day I first met Sadie appeared to be true: she was a special creature with a unique gift to share with the world. I had been so totally focused on what Sadie needed to "get" in order to stay alive—therapy, medicine, veterinary care, financial support, help with bodily functions—that I hadn't thought much about how much she could "give" to others. Maybe, though, it was time to start thinking.

I lay back in the long, lush grass, breathing in the soft sweet scent of soil and clover as dandelion leaves feathered against the side of my face. I reached for Sadie's head and rested her chin on my sternum, staring into her gentle amber eyes as she stretched her long front legs beside my ribs, flexing and curling her toes. "What do you think, girl?" I asked. "Do you have a special role in life that neither of us has realized yet?"

She didn't answer, other than a slight, twitching, "a fly may have landed on me" wag of her tail. Maybe I was tired, or maybe it was the low light, and don't hold me to it, but I could have sworn, at that moment, that Sadie winked at me.

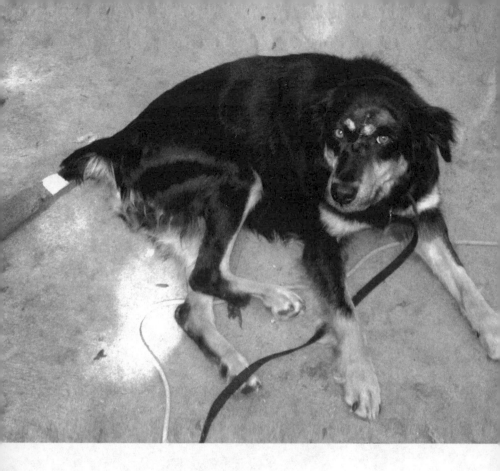

CHAPTER FIVE
Sadie Faces Surgery

Post-surgery.

A few days before Sadie's surgery to remove the bullet from her forehead and the cyst from her tail, I was on my way out of Dr. Jodie's clinic after having picked up a refill of Sadie's supplements. Sadie was still at swimming with my dog-sitter, Jeff, so for once I was on my own. A woman entering the clinic as I was exiting held the door open, ushering me past. "Thanks so much," I said and smiled. As we made eye contact, I was suddenly struck by how familiar the woman looked. Sixty-ish, blond, of average height and build and dressed in jeans and flowered blouse, she, too, stopped and stared as if she recognized me.

"Joal?" she asked.

"Yes . . ." I paused. "Karen?" *Of course.* Now I knew why she looked so familiar—it was Marnette's stepdaughter-in-law, Karen, who was married to Marnette's stepson, Rich. (Marnette's husband had been much older than she, so the children from his first marriage were close to Marnette's age.) I probably hadn't seen Karen in ten years, but I knew that Marnette had kept in touch with her even after Marnette's husband had died.

"What a surprise," Karen said, smiling widely. "You look terrific. And how is Sadie? How is she doing?" I wasn't surprised that Karen knew about Sadie; Marnette had probably told Karen about her, or Karen had received one of the many emails or website links that Marnette was regularly sending out, telling all about Sadie and her struggle to walk again.

Karen, who lived in Milwaukee, was an esoteric healer by profession. Esoteric healing is a type of holistic alternative therapy that aims to help people heal from physical and emotional disease and disability by focusing on their internal energy fields. Knowing this, I began to feel uncomfortable as Karen pressed me for information.

"Sadie is doing great," I replied breezily. "She's making progress every single day."

Karen nodded, but then suddenly her smile vanished. Her face became solemn, her eyes dark and serious.

"You know, Joal, animals are not like people," she said softly, glancing down and shaking her head. "When a dog dies, for example, it's not like a person dying. When a dog dies, its spirit simply moves on, transitioning to another realm, a realm where they are free of pain and suffering."

I started to panic. *Why is she telling me this?*

"People often have a hard time saying good-bye to the animals they love so much, but it would be easier if they tried not to think of an animal's death as being similar to a human passing away," she continued. "When a dog is put down, it isn't really like killing the animal, it is more like releasing the soul so it is free to go to a better place."

Oh my God—she's saying I should have Sadie put to sleep! Is that what Sadie wants? Whether she realized it or not, Karen was engaging one of my greatest fears. *Is Sadie in more pain and discomfort than I realize?*

I listened numbly as Karen continued talking. My head was spinning, and much of what she was saying, frankly, sounded like New Age mumbo-jumbo, but I was too taken aback, too stunned by her words to respond. I just wanted to rush home to Sadie, scoop her up in my arms, and make sure she was okay. But instead I just stood and listened, nodding occasionally. In my mind there was no doubt Karen believed that she was in touch with Sadie and that Sadie was telling her that she wanted to be released from this life so she could run free and unencumbered on that mystical "other side."

Karen probably spoke to me for twenty minutes or so, but I remember little else of what was said, other than her closing, which was, "Remember, Joal, dogs don't die like people do. When they leave us, it is very peaceful, and they go to a place where their souls are free and live in bliss forever."

I was still numb as we said our good-byes and I climbed into my SUV. I drove home on autopilot; it was fortunate that it was such a short drive since I could barely breathe through the thick lump in my throat, or see the road through my hot, furious tears. What if Karen was right? Personally, I didn't put much store in wacky New Age philosophies, but I also couldn't be sure that Karen *didn't* have a way to access parts of Sadie that I couldn't.

When I arrived home Jeff was there with Sadie, having just returned from swimming. I gave Sadie the biggest hug ever, then I took off her diaper and encouraged her to play in the grass. But she just sat there, withdrawn and vacant. "Come on, Sadie, let's play," I cajoled, tossing her one of her toys, a red rubber squeeze ball. She turned her head to watch the ball sail through the air, but she remained firmly planted in the grass. "Come on, Sadie, go for the ball." I went over and grabbed the ball, ducked and faked, moving my hand with the ball up and down and side to side. Still Sadie sat, tongue wagging, eyes staring aimlessly.

"C'mon, girl. Please? For me?" Like a flash, I experienced a sudden moment of insight in which I saw Sadie differently, at a distance and more objectively, from the perspective of someone not so emotionally involved. I had had Sadie for more than a month now; how much progress had she actually made? Hours of therapy and exercise, a special diet and supplements, and for what? "Okay, Sadie, maybe you're just not in the mood right now," I decided. "We'll try again later."

After saying good-bye to Jeff, I helped Sadie urinate, then cleaned her up, brought her inside, and gave her a clean diaper. Sparky greeted us with slobbery kisses and requests for treats while Miss Kitty and Kit Kat administered urgent head bumps and arched themselves against my legs, demanding attention. Meanwhile Sadie just sat, watching, head down, chin resting on her front paws. Hard as I tried, I just couldn't get the conversation with Karen out of my head. *Do I imagine Sadie is getting better because I want her to be better?* I wondered and worried. *Am I too blinded by love to see the truth?*

This was the worst I had felt since Sadie had entered my life. I was a mess, and my hands were shaking as I phoned Marnette and told her of my encounter with Karen. "I think she was saying that Sadie doesn't want to live," I explained, my voice breaking. "I think she was trying to tell me it was okay to let her go. Like she was giving me permission or something."

Marnette was furious when she heard this. Anyone who's

met Marnette knows she is a classy, elegant lady who has developed true Southern charm and grace after living in the South for so long, but she is also a cougar when it comes to protecting those she loves. Unsurprisingly, she leaped to my defense. "Don't listen to her, Joal," Marnette pleaded. "Karen doesn't know Sadie. She doesn't know you. Karen has never even seen Sadie in person, for goodness' sake! You are the one that Sadie speaks to; you are the one she communicates with, not Karen. Karen doesn't have any special insight into how Sadie is thinking or feeling. Trust Sadie. Trust your heart. Sadie will tell you what she wants and needs."

I sighed. "I know I shouldn't let Karen bother me," I agreed. "Her comments just caught me off guard, I guess. And I'm nervous about Sadie's surgery on Monday. I'm worried how she'll handle it."

"Of course. She's your baby now, and even minor surgery is scary," Marnette comforted. "But just remember how many people care about Sadie, how many people are praying for her every single day. Draw strength from that, Joal."

As I hung up the phone after talking to Marnette, I did feel a little better. There would probably always be people who didn't "get" Sadie, or who didn't approve of my putting so many resources into rescuing one disabled dog when there were so many other worthy causes in the world. But I couldn't think about those people or those causes at the moment. For now, my main job was to think about Sadie.

Monday, June 4, 2012, the day of Sadie's surgery, dawned warm, hazy, and humid, with storm clouds gathering on the horizon. My own mood was just as cloudy and unsettled. I hadn't slept much the night before, worrying about how Sadie would handle the anesthesia, the operation, the recovery. I kept peering over the side of my bed to see how she was doing, curled up on her dog bed on the floor. I'd taken her to the clinic the day before for her pre-surgery exam and blood work and everything had looked good. Still, as I lifted Sadie in my arms that morning and bundled her into the back of my SUV, I held her a little longer than necessary, kissing her lumpy forehead and pressing her close to my chest, then rocking her slightly, as you might a child, absorbing the full warm weight of her in my arms.

Since Dr. Jodie preferred to focus on holistic treatments for her patients, Sadie's actual surgery was going to be performed by Dr. Jodie's colleague, Dr. Witte. It wasn't even nine a.m. yet when I carried Sadie into the clinic, but the staff was busy and bustling as always, already well into their day. To an outsider, it would have looked like an ordinary morning in which I was dropping off Sadie for her treatments and therapy on my way to work. Looks, however, can be deceiving, because inside, I was a wreck. There was nothing ordinary about Sadie undergoing surgery.

Dr. Jodie's assistant Kati took Sadie from my arms and carried her into the back to start prepping her for surgery. I stayed behind at the front desk, signing consent forms. Included in the forms were questions about what type of CPR and other life-saving measures I was authorizing for Sadie, should something go terribly wrong (always a possibility with surgery and anesthesia). This paperwork was routine, just a formality, really, but still, it was sobering to think about those things and have to make those life-or-death decisions. *What if I make the wrong choice, or change my mind? How can I be sure what's really best for Sadie?*

Once the paperwork was finished, it was time to say good-bye to Sadie. She was in an exam room, stretched out on a table, an IV port already inserted into her front paw. I kissed her forehead, then rubbed it with my chin, feeling the bullet beneath the skin for what I hoped would be the final time. I would have preferred to have stayed at the clinic all day, close to Sadie in case she needed me, but really there was nothing I could do here but sit and wait; she'd spend most of the afternoon sleeping off the anesthetic. And considering my financial circumstances, I certainly couldn't afford to take a day off work; there are no paid sick days or personal days when you're self-employed.

As I climbed into my SUV and pulled out of the parking lot, I felt utterly bereft, desperately trying to think of something other than Sadie. The fear and helplessness I felt brought back traumatic memories of when my younger daughter, Jami-Lyn, was about three years old and developed a severe case of bronchiolitis, a serious viral infection of the bronchioles, the small air passageways in the lungs. My normally fair-skinned, steady, levelheaded toddler, always so cheerful and inquisitive, suddenly became stiff with fever, arching back and going rigid in my arms. Her skin was crimson and hot to the touch, as she screamed and sobbed, fighting for breath.

Frantic, my husband rushed us to the doctor's as I held Jami-Lyn in my arms in the backseat, rocking and praying and bargaining with God. "Please, God, protect my baby. Let her be okay." And to Jami-Lyn I cooed, "Hang on, sweetheart, Momma's got you now."

From the doctor's office we were sent straight to the hospital, where Jami-Lyn was torn from my arms and whisked off to an exam room. Once stabilized, she was admitted as a patient, placed in an oxygen tent, and given intense vaporizer treatments.

I refused to leave her bedside during those long, terrifying few days, willing her to breathe, watching her tiny chest rise and fall, unable to touch her or hold her through the plastic tent surrounding her hospital crib. It felt like the earth had stopped turning, suspended in time and space, until finally Jami-Lyn recovered enough to come home, and the world could kick into motion once more.

"You're being foolish, Joal," I told myself as I merged onto the highway, heading toward that day's job in Illinois. *Sadie isn't your child. She's just a dog, you know.* And yet deep down, I had to admit she was so much more than a dog to me now.

Fortunately, I was able to phone the clinic several times during the day while at work, getting periodic updates on Sadie's status. I was so relieved when I received word that the surgery was over and had gone well; both the bullet from her forehead and the cyst from her tail had been successfully removed and she was resting comfortably.

When at last work finished for the day and I rushed back to the clinic, Dr. Witte was with a patient so Dr. Jodie took me in to see Sadie. Poor Sadie! She was still quite groggy and barely seemed to recognize me as she slowly lifted her head from the pile of blankets surrounding her, and her amber eyes struggled to focus. The fur on her forehead had been shaved down to the skin and she had six or seven large green stitches closing an incision that went from above her eyebrows, between her eyes, and down to the base of her snout.

Dr. Jodie explained that the surgery hadn't taken long. The bullet was fairly close to the surface, thanks to the poultice, and hadn't gone into the bone. Then Dr. Jodie reached into her pocket and pulled out a cylindrical metal object.

"Here it is," she said, holding the object up to the light. "Fortunately, it hadn't fragmented and came out in one piece." A chill arced through me as I realized she was holding the bullet. To actually see it with my own eyes was shocking and sobering, bringing home the reality that Sadie had actually been shot, with a real gun and real bullets, and by a real human being who chose to do this to her.

Seeing the actual bullet made it so much more real. On one hand, I was glad to think that this cold, hard piece of metal was no longer embedded inside Sadie's body, but it also reminded me that the bullet and shrapnel in her back, those many pieces of cold, hard metal too numerous to count, could never be removed, and she would carry those cruel reminders of the worst day of her life inside of her forever.

Dr. Jodie continued by explaining that the surgery on the cyst had actually been more extensive than that on her forehead since the cyst was larger and deeper than suspected. They chose not to close the incision with stitches because it would heal better if left open, and as Dr. Jodie showed me the area, I was shocked to realize that so much tissue had been removed that I could see the tendons in Sadie's tail! How much more was this poor dog going to have to endure? I wondered.

"You'll need to let Sadie soak in the bathtub twice a day

for twenty minutes each time, then treat and re-bandage her tail," Dr. Jodie explained. "You'll need to do this for at least two weeks. And no more swimming for Sadie for at least a month, until her tail is fully healed."

"Wait a minute—you mean put her in *my* tub—the one in my bathroom?" I asked incredulously. About once a week I had been giving Sadie a full bath in the kiddie pool in the yard, while at least once a day I was "spot-washing" her, especially her back end, with rags and towels and a pitcher of water. No doubt Sadie and I had grown close, but I had never placed a dog in my own bathtub before and couldn't fathom starting now.

"Well, yes," Dr. Jodie replied, looking slightly annoyed as her brown eyes narrowed. "That would be the best way to do it, of course."

Fast-forward a few hours to that evening and there I was in my master bathroom, lifting Sadie from the floor, steadying her in my arms, and carefully lowering her into my bathtub filled with warm, soapy water. "I seriously hope you appreciate this," I told her as I wet a washcloth and began wiping her shoulders and chest. Still groggy from her surgery, she looked at me with hazy, melted-caramel eyes, but otherwise didn't react. I washed her gently, avoiding the stitches on her head, and once the bandage on her tail had been softened enough by the water, I cut it off with a pair of scissors and cleaned the open wound.

After taking her out of the tub and drying her, I laid Sadie on the floor and tried not to look at the exposed tendons as I treated her tail with the ointment Dr. Jodie had prescribed, which resembled a thick red Vaseline. Then I bandaged the wound as she had taught me, first wrapping it with gauze and then finishing with the black vet wrap that was thin, snug, and highly adhesive. Sadie was an ideal patient, as always, never barking or nipping or complaining. She would just lie on her side and look up at me, doe-eyed and placid, as if biding her time until I was finished.

So, twice a day for two weeks, I bathed Sadie in my bathtub and let her soak for twenty minutes, before and after work. This became just another element that was added to our morning and evening routine, which now included outdoor potty time on her own, diaper changes, feedings, supplements, and exercises, along with the twenty-minute baths. Sometimes I felt overwhelmed and exhausted by the sheer time and energy all this took. But in those moments, I would tell myself, *Be strong and stay the course. Remember, you're doing this for Sadie. It won't always be this way; it won't be like this forever. When her tail heals, when she's stronger, when she's better, when she's walking again . . .*

During these intense weeks of bathing and healing, I was greatly anticipating a five-day trip to Louisville, Kentucky, to attend the national convention of the RROC—the Rolls-Royce Owners' Club, Lake Michigan region. Cars have always been one of my passions; I've been a "car guy" since the age of fourteen, even before I learned to drive. I was fortunate enough to have been elected to the club's board of directors, and was so looking forward to the national convention and the trip to Louisville, including a side trip to Churchill Downs, famous home of the Kentucky Derby.

The trip to Kentucky had been scheduled well before I adopted Sadie, and the travel and accommodations had already been paid for. I had really hoped I could go, hoped that Sadie would be well enough that Jeff could keep her overnight and drop her off at Dr. Jodie's during the day. I was excited about getting a break and the chance to rest and recharge my batteries, but as the days went on, it was becoming more and more evident that I couldn't leave Sadie. Although healing, she was still in rough shape, and I knew the intense rehab schedule we'd been sticking to couldn't be compromised or interrupted.

So it was with a heavy heart that I called my friends from the club and told them I wouldn't be able to make the trip to Kentucky after all because Sadie needed me too much. They were supportive and seemed to take the news well, but deep down I wondered if they thought I was crazy for canceling a trip because of my dog. My family, other than my stalwart supporter Marnette, were struggling to accept how much Sadie had taken over my life—was I at risk of losing my friends now, too?

It was a week after Sadie's surgery and we were at Dr. Jodie's for a follow-up appointment. Both incisions were healing nicely and Sadie seemed to be on the mend. But then Dr. Jodie dropped a bombshell.

"Joal, it doesn't look as if we'll be able to do the amputation next month like we had hoped," she said sadly, running her hand along Sadie's spine. "Her right back leg is just not getting strong enough to support her."

My mind reeled. How was that possible? Sadie hadn't been swimming for a week since the surgery, to allow her tail to heal, but she was receiving acupuncture once a week, intense laser treatments on her back for pain relief, essential oil baths, and deep tissue massage several times a week, along with the diet, exercise, and supplements she was getting from me at home.

"The problem isn't the leg itself," Dr. Jodie continued, "it's more likely the spinal column. She just doesn't have enough nerve function in her lower back and legs. The damage caused by the bullet must be deeper and more extensive than we realized."

I felt as if my heart had stopped. "Are you telling me she'll never walk again?" My words tumbled out in a harsh whisper. Everything I'd done for the past month and a half, since I first found Sadie, had been focused on getting her walking again. *How can we give up now?*

"I'm not necessarily saying she'll never walk again," Dr. Jodie continued. "Nerves can regenerate over time. The process is very slow, but it can happen. But I don't believe amputation will ever be the solution for Sadie, because I don't think her back right leg will ever be strong enough to support her body. But there's still a chance that both back legs working together, even if compromised, could become strong enough to allow her to walk. So let's make her rehab even more aggressive and then see where she is in another month."

"Okay," I said softly, "if that's what you think best."

I was still numb and in shock as I bundled Sadie up and took her home. After giving Sadie a potty break followed by a fresh diaper, I made one of the toughest phone calls of my life, to Joanie, the woman who'd earlier offered us her dog's Walkin' Wheels.

"Hello, this is Joal Derse Dauer," I said, trying to steady my crackling voice when Joanie answered the phone. "We spoke about a month ago, regarding your Walkin' Wheels and my dog Sadie. I'd like to take you up on your offer, if the wheels are still available." I paused and swallowed hard. "Looks like we're going to be needing them after all."

Joanie seemed surprised but sympathetic, and we quickly arranged the details for delivery. I hung up the phone feeling an overwhelming mixture of sorrow, grief, disappointment, and, the swift current flowing steadily beneath all else, resolve. Sadie was perched patiently at my feet, looking up at me inquisitively, and I knelt down beside her, wrapping my arms around her shoulders and burying my face in her neck, letting the silky black-and-tan fur absorb my flowing tears.

"Sadie, you *are* going to walk again, I promise," I whispered into her floppy ear as she dropped her head and licked the back of my hand. "It might not be exactly the way we first imagined, but you *will* walk again, I just know it."

CHAPTER SIX

Sadie and Noah—
When Kindred Souls
Connect

"Come on, Sadie. Give it a try. Please? Do it for me. Come on, girl." I was kneeling on the floor in Dr. Jodie's exam room, along with vet tech Kati, eye to eye and nose to snout with a very stubborn and recalcitrant Sadie, who utterly, absolutely, unequivocally refused to follow my commands. "Please, Sadie? For me?" I begged.

The normally relaxed, calming mood of the room, with its low lighting, gentle music, and warm, subtle aroma of essential oils wafting above our heads, was today rife with tension as an uneasy stalemate, a tense détente, continued between mom and dog. It was Sadie's first time trying the Walkin' Wheels, and she was making it abundantly clear she wanted nothing to do with this contraption, even though it was a lightweight, streamline piece of equipment. The two wheels were situated at the back, alongside Sadie's legs, and the aluminum frame that bracketed the outside of her torso was attached via canvas-and-Velcro straps that circled her back and her chest.

"Come on, Sadie, just give it a try," I pleaded, gently grasping her shoulders and tugging her forward. "I promise it'll feel just like you're walking again." She whined in response and then collapsed her front legs beneath her body, staunchly locking them into place as her back end shot straight up into the air. There would be no moving her now.

"Why are you doing this to me?" I moaned. I felt as if my

beautiful, compliant, good-natured dog had suddenly transformed into a defiant toddler, mired deep in the depths of the "terrible twos."

"Well, I don't think it's hurting her," Kati offered, crossing her legs and tucking her long brown hair behind her ear.

"I don't think so, either," I agreed, sitting back on my heels and shaking my head. "I don't think Sadie's in pain. It's more like she finds the wheels . . . humiliating or something."

"Maybe it's just uncomfortable because she hasn't stood up and walked for so long," Kati suggested. "Maybe she's not familiar with those sensations anymore."

"That could be it," I replied, scratching my chin. "I figured the wheels would take some getting used to and she might not take to them right away," I added, trying not to sound as disappointed as I felt. My plan was to put Sadie in the wheels twice a week for thirty minutes at a time and build up her usage from there as she got stronger and more comfortable with the device. But Sadie was letting us know after only a few minutes that she clearly had had enough for today.

I motioned for Kati to help me get Sadie out of the wheels, and together we loosened the straps and released the frame. "All right, Sadie, at least you gave it a try." I stroked her head, offered her a treat, and gave her plenty of conciliatory kisses. I didn't want her to think that I was angry with her, or that she had let me down. I understood that encouragement was the best method for effecting change.

"We've still got your wagon," I reminded her. "And right now you need love and comfort more than you need your own wheels to get around. We'll try it again in a few days and see how you do then." As had happened so many times before, I had to remind myself that Sadie had her own internal schedule that only she was privy to; I couldn't make her stick to "my" schedule, no matter how hard I tried. She would walk again when she was good and ready to, and not a moment before.

Nearly two weeks had passed since Sadie's surgery. She had had the stitches taken out of her forehead a few days earlier and I could tell that her head was feeling much better. Her tail was healing, too, although that had clearly hurt much worse than her head. I wrapped, treated, cleaned, and rewrapped the incision on her tail twice a day, and I could see the wound slowly but surely beginning to close over, knitting together with new tissue.

I was also still soaking Sadie in my bathtub twice a day for twenty to thirty minutes at a time, but I had started adding lavender oil to the bath, and Sadie absolutely loved the calming, soothing power of its gentle aroma. She actually fell asleep now while I bathed her, each and every time!

The one major concern I had during this period, and it worried me a lot, was that Sadie's mobility, such as it was, had dramatically decreased since the surgery. Although I had never seen her "walk" prior to her surgery, she had been doing her "bunny hop" more and more, with more strength, longer duration, and greater distance covered. But now it seemed like her good right leg had weakened, and neither Dr. Jodie nor I could figure out why. Perhaps the strength would come back in time, but I sure wasn't willing to wait and risk it getting even worse. Something dramatic needed to happen immediately, so I made an appointment to have

Sadie evaluated at TOPS Veterinary Rehabilitation center, about sixty miles away in Grayslake, Illinois.

One of the few, not to mention one of the best, rehab centers in the country devoted solely to treating animals, TOPS offered state-of-the-art therapies including hydrotherapy, ultrasound, cryotherapy, acupuncture, chiropractic, massage, and several other treatment protocols. I was familiar with TOPS because I had taken some of my other animals for treatment there in the past. If anyone could help Sadie get her rehab back on track so she could focus on walking again, it was the vets, techs, and therapists at TOPS.

So on June 18, 2012, I bundled Sadie into the back of my SUV and together we made the hour-long drive down to Grayslake, a leafy, affluent village about forty miles north of Chicago. Sadie's team that day was led by Dr. Lisa Starr and treatment supervisor Cassandra Sorenson. They began their assessment of Sadie by tying a towel around her midsection to support her and then holding her up while she was placed on a long carpet and encouraged to walk. She did in fact take a few steps, but only backward!

No matter what we tried, Sadie made no attempt to propel herself forward. None of us could figure out why. Was this simply her way of dealing with back legs that couldn't hold her up? Whatever the reason, the stubborn Sadie I had encountered when I tried to get her to use the Walkin' Wheels surfaced yet again as she absolutely refused to move forward. This was frustrating, of course, but I rejoiced in a small corner of my soul to think that the passive, vacant, empty-eyed Sadie that I'd adopted less than two months earlier was now, more and more frequently, showing signs of defiance, determination, and good old-fashioned spunk. *That's my Sadie*, I thought proudly, *my stubborn baby girl*, as they undid the towel around her middle and released her, and she fumbled, tumbled, and stumbled straight into my waiting arms.

Following Sadie's assessment, Dr. Lisa and her team recommended Sadie attend TOPS twice a week to receive treatment including chiropractic, cranial-sacral therapy, passive range of motion, e-stim (neuromuscular stimulation via electrical current), and TOPS's unique hydro-treadmill, the first and only underwater treadmill in the world exclusively for use with dogs. The warmth of the water combined with the lack of weight would make it easier for Sadie to move and to strengthen her legs. The machine also included underwater cameras that projected the images onto a screen, so the vets could observe and evaluate Sadie's gait in real time. The TOPS staff recommended that Sadie continue this intensive treatment regimen until the end of October, or, in other words, for about four and a half months, to yield the best results.

This all sounded amazing, and amazingly expensive. We were still receiving donations online at a steady pace, but the amounts given were small (although always deeply appreciated). The money I had stocked away in savings and retirement funds was dwindling quickly and meanwhile Sadie seemed to be further away from walking than ever before. Still, what could I do? I had come too far with her, and had too much faith that she would walk again someday, to quit now. If I gave up on Sadie, then all this had truly been for nothing. And I couldn't very well ask her just to remain in her diminished state, consigned to only moving via short, painful bunny hops or dragging her lifeless back legs on the ground behind her because that was all I could afford.

Sadie did not deserve the cruel hand she'd been dealt in life. I assumed her only "crime" was to continually give birth to litters of puppies for her owner, until she was no longer needed, and then they shot her in the head and abandoned her in the woods to die. Sadie desperately deserved a second chance in life, and I was determined to be the one who gave it to her.

The reality was that as much as I had tried not to, I had fallen deeply, desperately, head over heels in love with Sadie. She was my "dog-ter" now, and I was her forever mom. We were in this together, through thick and thin. So I would just have to find a way to tighten my belt, cut costs, and do without. If that's what it was going to take to save Sadie, that's exactly what I was going to do.

I've written quite a bit about all the therapies and treatments that Sadie was receiving during the summer of 2012, but it might be helpful here to describe them in more detail, to give a clearer picture of how intensive Sadie's rehab was during that period and how hard we were all working to get her back on her feet, literally and metaphorically. A typical week at that time looked something like this:

At TOPS Veterinary Rehab in Grayslake, Illinois
(twice a week, Mondays and Fridays; a round-trip two-hour drive):
Hydro-Treadmill—twenty minutes on the treadmill in the pool, trying to get her legs to support her body, take forward steps, and work in unison

Hako-Med Pool—therapeutic soaking for pain management

Chiropractic—to improve the alignment of Sadie's spine, pelvis, and legs

Cranial-sacral Massage—hands-on manipulation of her skull and spine

Passive Range of Motion Therapy—exercises to improve joint mobility

e-stim—Neuromuscular stimulation via electrical current

At the Animal Doctor Holistic Veterinary Complex in Muskego, Wisconsin
(three days a week, Tuesday, Wednesday, Thursday, from 9 a.m. to 5 p.m.)

Acupuncture (once a week)—inserting dry needles into specific points on the body to improve blood flow and increase nerve regeneration

Aqua puncture—injecting small amounts of liquids such as vitamin B12 or homeopathic remedies into acupuncture points

Laser treatment—using a small, handheld device to emit an intense beam of deeply penetrating laser light to provide pain relief

Essential oil baths—for relaxation

Full-body massage—deep tissue massage to increase blood flow and stimulate muscles

Physical therapy—targeted exercises to improve strength, agility, mobility, and balance

At-home Therapy, Treatment, Exercise
(seven days a week, mornings and evenings, two to three hours per session, four to six hours per day)

Swimming—to build strength and endurance; twenty-minute sessions, two to three times a week at Think Pawsitive (once tail incision had healed)

Raw meat diet—to ease elimination and build muscle

Supplements—to build strength

Massage therapy—stimulation and relaxation with a hand-held massager

Trampoline—to improve balance and coordination and strengthen Sadie's legs

Power Plate—to increase strength and nerve function

Peanut ball—to stretch and exercise hamstring muscles

e-stim—to encourage cell growth and regeneration

I had no training, background, or personal experience in physical education, physical therapy, or animal rehabilitation, but I was determined to do everything I could to get Sadie walking again, so I became creative in terms of what types of exercises and activities I could do with her at home to complement and supplement what she was already getting at TOPS and at Dr. Jodie's.

Take, for example, the trampoline. This was just a little round one-person trampoline that I had used as part of my own exercise routine to stay in shape, but now I started taking Sadie on it with me. I would hold her up so she was standing between my legs with all four paws on the trampoline. Once we were balanced and steady, I would slowly and gently shift my weight from left to right, then right to left, feeling the slight movement in the trampoline, and Sadie reacted by also shifting her weight in response, thus activating and engaging the atrophied muscles in her hindquarters and back legs.

The Power Plate, meanwhile, was a whole-body vibration apparatus that was designed to activate the body's natural reflex response to vibration. I had been using it as part of my workout routine for many years. Originally devised by the Russians for use by athletes and cosmonauts, the stand-up machine has at its base a metal platform that can be set to vibrate at various high-speed frequencies at thirty- and sixty-second intervals, with a period of rest in between. As you stand on the plate, the intense vibration engages all the body's muscles in a controlled and consistent manner. The machine can also be used to specifically target the arms, legs, or other parts of the body.

I knew there was no way Sadie would have the strength, balance, or stability to stand with all four paws on the rectangular, rapidly vibrating plate, so I got creative. I devised a way that I could hold Sadie's hips and legs on the plate while her front paws stood on the lid of a large plastic tote box positioned on the floor in front of the plate. This way her back legs and her front legs remained at an equal height. At first Sadie could only tolerate a few turns on the machine at a time, but I believed that using the machine would help stimulate the nerves and muscles in her back and legs.

The "peanut ball" was a peanut-shaped exercise ball that I used to loosen and lengthen the ligaments in Sadie's back legs by having her gently stretch and roll the ball beneath her hindquarters. As Dr. Jodie had noticed the first time I brought Sadie in for evaluation, when Sadie tried to walk, her back left leg curled under and in, beneath her body, crossing in front of the other legs and hindering her movement. The hope was that by stretching, loosening, and lengthening those ligaments, her back legs would straighten out and thus be better able to support her body.

In terms of the e-stim, the electronic stimulation treatments that Sadie was receiving at TOPS, it was quite expensive to have those treatments done by a therapist, so in my ongoing commitment to cutting costs and saving money, I went online and purchased my own e-stim machine so I could do Sadie's treatments myself at home. This was surprisingly easy once Sadie had been shaved in strategic locations so the pads that were attached to wire leads would conduct the electricity more easily through her skin than by having to pass through Sadie's thick fur.

The e-stim machine, a small, handheld device, uses an electrical current to stimulate the muscles to expand and contract, much like exercise, but passively rather than actively. The machine could be set at various Hertz frequencies. We used it at 25 Hertz for some locations on Sadie's body and 50 Hertz on others, usually for twenty minutes at each location. I learned I had to be very careful about how much of this treatment Sadie could tolerate. I did these treatments on her three times a week, and I had to allow an hour for each session, which further added to my already ex-hausting and time-consuming Sadie rehab schedule.

By now it was the last week of June and Marnette was scheduled to visit in a few days, meeting Sadie in person for the very first time. I wondered what she would think of this crazy schedule that I'd created for Sadie and me. Although Marnette had been nothing but supportive since Sadie came into our lives, devoting serious time, money, energy, and sheer hard work toward the Saving Sadie effort, it would be different for her actually witnessing the entire op-eration up close. Would she worry about the toll all this was taking on me, physically, emotionally, financially? Would she think the whole thing was too overwhelming, too intense, too indulgent, too expensive? Would she come to believe that it—that Sadie—wasn't worth it?

Although I had serious concerns, I also couldn't wait for Marnette to get here. Rehabbing a disabled dog can be a lonely and isolating undertaking, and as much as I loved my fur babies, it would be wonderful to have human compan-ionship once again.

Marnette arrived on Saturday, June 30. I drove to the air-port to pick up Marnette with Sadie and Sparky riding along in the back of the SUV. When I opened the back hatch to put Marnette's suitcase inside, her eyes met Sadie's and it was truly a case of love at first sight.

"Oh Joal, she's beautiful!" she exclaimed. "The photos don't do her justice." She reached in toward Sadie, and Sadie, with her best "I'm trying as hard as I can" little wag of her tail, stretched toward Marnette. What followed was a mini-love-fest of petting, stroking, ear rubs, and cuddles.

"She's just wonderful." Marnette sighed, her blue eyes shining with tears. "I'm so glad you didn't give up on her."

I had taken the week off work for Marnette's visit, and she became my shadow as we did all of Sadie's activities together, from feeding and bathing her to driving her to TOPS in Illinois to acupuncture at Dr. Jodie's to exercises on the trampoline, peanut ball, and Power Plate. After a few days, I could see Marnette was feeling the fatigue, but I still wasn't sure what she thought of Project Saving Sadie overall. She had been very observant of everything, but withheld any judgment.

"So is it all more than you thought it would be?" We were sitting together in the gazebo after dinner, sharing a bottle of Viognier as we enjoyed the soft summer evening breeze. I swallowed hard and poured myself another glass of wine. "Do you think it's too much, all this work to get Sadie walking again?"

She thought for a moment, then set down her glass. "I am amazed by what you're doing," she replied. "Sadie is extraordinary, and the experience of seeing all this in person has opened my heart even wider than before." She reached down and stroked Sadie, who was curled up contentedly at her feet.

"Before I came here I only had your description of how Sadie goes to the bathroom, how you carry her outside, hold her abdomen and massage her while she urinates, and then clean her up afterward. But now I have observed it with my own eyes. I see you soaking Sadie in your bathtub, in your own bathroom, then cutting the bandage off her tail, treating the wound, and re-bandaging it. I see how you feed her, how you give her her medicine, mixing it with raw meat and feeding her each individual pill inside the meat, from a paper plate with a special fork." She paused to reach for her wineglass.

"I see you driving to Illinois, an hour drive each way, twice a week, so Sadie can rehab at TOPS," she continued. "And I know you are too proud to admit it, but clearly you are sacrificing; you are going without in terms of your own needs, just so you can better provide for Sadie."

"I'm only doing it because I love Sadie so much," I whispered, my voice cracking. I realized this was the first time I had admitted it to anyone other than myself. "I so want her to be able to walk again."

"And she *will* walk again," Marnette insisted. "Because you, Joal, do not take no for an answer. Do you have any idea how inspiring you are?"

I blanched. "Me? Inspiring?"

"Yes. You are an inspiration. Not just to me, but to everyone who meets you and Sadie, or reads about the two of you online or in the media. It's a miracle, what's happening here. My sister adopted this pitiful creature, just a helpless ball of fur curled up on the ground, and look what she's got now. And this is still just the beginning. I know that Sadie was sent to us for a reason." Marnette stroked Sadie's head, and Sadie, as if she understood, responded with a happy little bark.

I twirled the stem of my wineglass between my fingertips. "I sometimes wonder," I began slowly, "do you think Mom and Dad would be proud of me? Proud of what I'm doing?" We had endured such a difficult adolescence, and I was still just in my early twenties when our parents passed away. It was only with Marnette that I could talk about these things. She understood because she had lived the sorrow, too.

"I *know* they would be proud," she insisted. "Joal, you have always been someone who never gives up once you set your mind to something. I still remember you as a little girl, teaching yourself how to ice-skate. You cleared all the snow off that pond at Whitnall Park and then practiced figure skating like you were training for the Olympics. You were trying to master turning on one blade so you just did it, over and over again. No matter how many times you fell, you just got right back up again." She smiled at the memory. "Mom and Dad would be proud of you." She paused. "But no prouder than I am right now."

Friday, July 6, the day before Marnette was leaving, was the second Jammin' on Janesville, following the first one a month earlier in June. If anything, July's Jammin' on Janesville was even busier than the previous one, and Marnette reveled in the live music, the crowds, the food, the nonstop party atmosphere that filled block after block of Janesville Road.

Marnette joined Sadie and me at our station at the booth in front of Dr. Jodie's clinic, greeting visitors and handing out Sadie's business card to everyone who passed by. I was humbled and amazed by how many people were coming to see Sadie again after having met her at the last Jammin', and how many people were seeing her for the first time, determined to meet "that amazing dog" in person after reading about her in the newspaper or online. It looked like all of our intense outreach efforts were finally starting to pay off, as people asked to meet "the famous Sadie."

Sadie, for her part, was an absolute star once again, showing no fear, irritation, or fatigue as she sat up, tall and steady in her Little Tikes green plastic wagon, a yellow bandanna knotted jauntily around her neck, as grown-ups poked and stroked and petted her, and inquisitive children squealed and grabbed on to her fur, asking all kinds of questions about what was wrong with her, why she couldn't walk, and so on. In the midst of all this, a petite, fortysomething woman with long blond hair approached me, introduced herself as Lisa, and asked if her friend and patient, Noah, could say hello to Sadie.

Noah was a towering African American man in his mid-thirties, with a muscular build and trim mustache and beard. His deep-set dark brown eyes looked lost and vacant, filled with inexpressible sorrow. I sensed immediately that Noah had some special needs and would do better in a more private setting, engaging with Sadie one on one without all the noise and commotion of the street fair. So, leaving Marnette to man our station, I pulled Sadie in her wagon to a quiet, shady corner beside the clinic and away from the road, with Lisa and Noah following close behind.

"Hello, Noah. I'm Joal," I said, looking into his eyes and smiling once we had found a good spot to talk. I lifted Sadie out of her wagon and laid her in the grass. Then I sat down beside her and motioned for Noah to sit as well. "This is Sadie," I said gently. "She likes it when you pet her. See?" I ran my hand over Sadie's head and down her back to demonstrate. Shyly at first, Noah reached out and patted Sadie's head, then touched her head again and let his hand rest

Joal and Sadie *(photo courtesy Valerie Alba)*

Marnette and Sadie *(author photo*

(author photo

In harness for transfer
to therapy pool
(author photo)

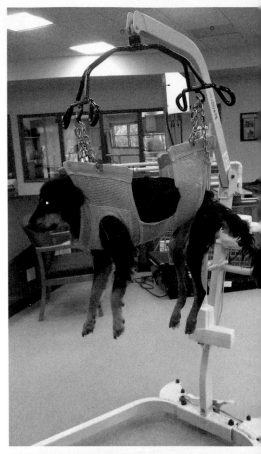

Air splints for therapy
(author photo)

(author photo)

(photo courtesy Valerie Alba)

Unhappy about swimming *(author photo)*

Unhappy after swimming *(author photo)*

Sadie's re-birthday celebration with Sparky, Mya, and George *(author photo)*

(author photo)

At Whitewater 5K Run
with Kim Becker (left)
and Mary Schultz
(author photo)

With Jeff Ziglinski
(author photo)

With Dr. Jodie Gruenstern
(author photo)

(author photo)

(photo courtesy Valerie Alba)

At Milwaukee Pride Parade *(photo courtesy Valerie Alba)*

Sadie salutes the
Fourth of July
(author photo)

(author photo)

Reading *Ruff Guide to the United States* by BringFido.com *(author photo)*

Sadie's logo on Muskego Police Canine Unit cruiser *(author photo)*

(author photo)

With Valerie Alba at the
GAB anti-bullying event
(author photo)

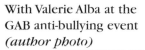

(photo courtesy C-Elise Photography)

there a moment longer. Sadie, for her part, seemed mesmerized, looking right at Noah, staring into his haunted brown
eyes with a kind of recognition as she drank in his attention.

As Noah and Sadie bonded, Lisa sat down in the grass beside me and told me Noah's story. Six years earlier, in 2006,
Noah had been working for a defense contractor in Iraq, at
the height of the Iraq War, when he'd suffered a traumatic
brain injury after being shot by a sniper. Noah had been riding in a truck as part of a convoy when a bullet from an AK-
47 entered through his right ear and ended up lodged deep
in the center of his brain, where it could not be removed.

"Noah was flown back to the U.S. on life support and not
expected to survive," Lisa continued. "He's had multiple
surgeries and infections, too many to count. He still has
some right-side paralysis and language issues, but he has
learned to walk again and his speech is improving. He's
made amazing progress, but he still has a really long and
rough road ahead of him." Lisa explained that she was a registered nurse who owned a place called Acres of Hope and
Aspirations, a small farm and rehabilitation center nearby
where Noah was just one of many people she was working
with to overcome brain injuries and disabilities.

With tears in my eyes, I excused myself for a moment and
went to get Marnette from the booth out front, telling her
she had to come see what I was seeing. When we returned
to the quiet space beside the building, Sadie was stretched
out in the grass between Lisa and Noah. Lisa, arms circling
her knees, was beaming, and Noah, this gentle giant of a
man who had endured so much, was petting Sadie very
gently from head to tail and speaking soft words that only

the two of them could understand. Two damaged, troubled souls had reached out, each finding healing in the other.

"This is absolutely incredible," I whispered to Marnette, shaking my head as goose bumps rose and a chill danced down my spine. "Noah was shot in the head and had to learn to walk again. Sadie was shot in the head and is learning to walk again. They have a bond. It's like they speak the same language, like they understand each other."

"That's because they do understand each other," Marnette insisted. "I told you a few days ago that I believe Sadie was sent to us for a reason. I think we're seeing that reason in action, right here and now. This is Sadie's gift to the world. There's no limit to what she can achieve." She smiled warmly and gave me a knowing wink. "But it's up to us to make it happen."

CHAPTER SEVEN
Acres and Acres of Hope

Watching the way Sadie interacted with Noah, I knew Marnette was right: Sadie had a very special gift to share with the world. But I still wasn't sure exactly what form that gift would take, or how to bring it to fruition. I was working forty hours a week and Sadie was rehabbing a lot more than forty hours a week—how could we find the time, money, energy, and resources to do anything more than we were doing now?

True, there were events such as Jammin' on Janesville, where Sadie could meet and interact with people, spreading her message of hope, love, and second chances, and we had been contacted by several businesses and organizations that wanted to set up meet-and-greets with Sadie. *But how can we go bigger?* I wondered. *How can we take this further and be more proactive, more organized, and reach more people?* In my mind, the only way was to first get Sadie fully rehabbed and back on her feet. Then, once her treatments, therapy, and basic everyday care were less intensive and less time-consuming, we could focus not just on raising her profile in order to generate financial and other support, but on spreading Sadie's special message far and wide. *We'll get there, girl*, I promised her. *But for now, it's all about getting you better.*

* * *

As the summer of 2012 progressed, so did Sadie. She was becoming stronger, more confident, and more alert and energetic by the day. Fur sprouted on her forehead, in dark little tufts around where the stitches had been, and you had to look closely even to see that she'd had an operation. Her tail wound, since it was much bigger, was taking longer to heal, but even that was looking better and better by the day. Her therapy, treatment, and rehab continued in earnest, and we were never short of suggestions and recommendations for new things to try. For example, one of Sadie's followers sent us an illustration of a dog with numbered points located on various parts of the body, along with instructions on how to do Jin Shin Jyutsu, an alternative therapy designed to "harmonize the life energy in the body" by using one's fingers to hold and release the body's blocked energy points.

We also added more massage, now with a massage therapist for humans who had extended her practice to working on animals, too. I was open to trying anything and everything, as long as it didn't harm Sadie, of course, figuring we would never know what treatment, therapy, or procedure would provide that major breakthrough we were hoping and praying for, until we saw it in action.

Things were going so well that I was taken totally by surprise when I experienced my first serious "Sadie meltdown." It was a hot, hazy Saturday afternoon in early August and I had been working with Sadie for hours, on the Power Plate, the peanut ball, the trampoline, and some new indoor exercises I had come up with, trying to train her to use her legs to climb the stairs from the living room up to the bedrooms on her own. I would place a small piece of food on every other step, and the idea was that Sadie would have to lift herself from one step to the next to get the next piece of food.

I was behind her on the stair, supporting her rump while she reached forward with her front paws. We had gone up two steps, very slowly and awkwardly, but now she had stopped, all forty-plus pounds of her, and was absolutely refusing to move.

"Come on, Sadie," I coaxed, giving her a stronger and more pointed push. "Just one more step for me, okay?" I pushed again, bracing my back and straining my muscles as sweat poured down my forehead. Sadie plopped down on the step and folded her front legs beneath her. The gauntlet had been thrown down; clearly, she had no intention of moving.

"Fine. Have it your way!" I snapped, sliding my arms beneath her belly, lifting her up, and placing her back on the living room carpet at the base of the stairs. "Why can't you just do what I want? Why?" Tears sprang to my eyes, just a trickle at first, but then the dam burst. "Sadie, don't you see that I'm trying to help you?" I sobbed. "I just want you to be able to walk again."

My frustration really had nothing to do with trying to help her climb the stairs, I quickly realized. My meltdown was because here we were in August, I had had Sadie for a little more than three months, and, even with all the progress she'd made, she was nowhere close to where I thought she'd be by now. Sadie was still in a diaper and wasn't urinating when and how I wanted her to, she wasn't standing on her own, and she definitely wasn't walking.

"How much more do we have to do?" I cried out loud. I sank to the bottom step and sat with my face buried in my hands, letting the tears flow around my fingers. "Why isn't this working?"

Suddenly I felt a cold, wet nudge against my arm. Then another one, more insistent this time. I looked up and it was Sadie, trying to get my attention. She smiled her doggy smile and wagged her tail. I stroked her head, rubbing the base of her ears. Her bright, caramel-brown eyes gazed at me, full of love and optimism, as if to say, "Please don't be mad at me, Mom. I'm doing the best I can. It's really hard to get my legs to work the way we want them to."

"I know, girl, I know. I'm so sorry." I pulled her close, kissed her forehead, and wrapped my arms around her shoulders, letting the thick, soft fur around her neck absorb my tears. I realized that I was probably just stressed, overly tired, and in desperate need of a break. It wasn't fair to take my frustrations out on Sadie, so I phoned my dog-sitter, Jeff, and asked if he would come and take Sadie for the day. "I'll do better than that," he promised over the phone, and I could hear the smile in his voice. "Pack an overnight bag for Sadie and I'll bring her back tomorrow morning."

I hung up the phone with a sigh of relief. Jeff to the rescue. Slightly built and soft-spoken with short brown hair and glasses, Jeff, along with Marnette and Dr. Jodie, had become a vitally important member of Team Sadie. A Vietnam War veteran now dealing with very serious health problems, Jeff and I first met years ago, back in the 1980s when he, his ex-wife, and I were all members of a Corvette Club in Milwaukee. (Yep, that's me, always into cars!)

When I moved to Illinois we lost contact, but then I ran into him at a club reunion in the early 2000s and after that we kept in touch. By the time I moved back to Wisconsin in 2007, Jeff had retired, and he began pet-sitting for me, taking care of Sparky, Kit Kat, and Presley, the other dog I had at the time, when I was working out of town or had jobs that kept me gone from morning until night. When Sadie came into the picture, Jeff stepped up and quickly became my "right-hand man," driving Sadie to swimming when I was at work, and helping out whenever there were scheduling or other conflicts.

After Jeff came and picked up Sadie, I took a long, much-needed nap. Afterward I felt somewhat better, but still not my normal self. The despair and exhaustion I felt was bone-deep, seeping into the very core of my being. That night I went to sleep at seven thirty and woke up several times during the night, agonizing about why I felt so depressed and frustrated over a helpless animal. I loved Sadie, and I knew she was doing the best she could.

One of Sadie's many gifts to me is her teaching me about patience, I thought. *And today, I was a very bad pupil. But another of her gifts is hope and perseverance— I will try again and I will do better tomorrow. Sadie is always working on me, even when I'm least aware of it. She is pushing and prodding and challenging me, forcing my heart and my soul to grow bigger, more open, and more embracing than ever before.*

After that I fell into a deep, refreshing, dreamless sleep, with the whisper of a prayer for Sadie still on my lips as I snuggled under the covers with Sparky, Miss Kitty, and Kit

Kat. I realized how much I missed Sadie, how much it hurt not to have her sleeping on the dog bed on the floor beside my bed, hearing her occasional grumbles in the night. Our family was not complete without Sadie present, and we could never be whole without her here.

When Jeff brought Sadie home later the next morning, I threw my arms around her and covered her in kisses. "I know that sometimes I need to be patient with you, Sadie," I told her, "but sometimes, you'll have to be patient with me, too." She replied with a little bark, and a bigger-than-ever wag of her tail.

Throughout the summer of 2012 we were generating a lot of media coverage online for Sadie and for her story. Laura Simpson of the Great Animal Rescue Chase was regularly posting articles about Sadie on her websites and also on the Care2.com website, and dozens of people were sharing links to our articles, website, and social media sites. This was all wonderful, but I knew we needed more coverage from traditional media—TV, radio, magazines, and newspapers—if we were going to garner the kind of support we needed for Sadie long term.

Fortunately, around this time, my friend Robert Ritholz sent me an article from the *Daily Herald*, a newspaper out of Arlington Heights, Illinois, covering the northern and western suburbs of Chicago. The article mentioned our mutual friend, Jack Taylor, who was a radio announcer on WGN many years ago and a beloved TV anchorman on the five- and ten-o'clock Channel 9 news in Chicago. Jack was going to be hosting a new show called *A Few Minutes with Jack*

Taylor on Saturdays on WDCB, a public radio station owned by the College of DuPage in Illinois. Sensing an opportunity here, I decided to give Jack a call.

Jack, who is such a polite and funny gentleman, was happy to hear from me and listened intently as I told him all about how I had met, fallen in love, and adopted Sadie, a dog with special needs, and then asked him if there was anything he could do to help me spread the word about Sadie's plight. He immediately offered his assistance.

The first two connections Jack arranged didn't pan out, but then he put me in touch with Jamie Sotonoff at the *Herald*, who put me in touch with Burt Constable, the *Herald*'s seasoned reporter and columnist, and Burt asked to interview Sadie and me! The local connection for the *Daily Herald*'s readership was that Sadie received rehab at TOPS in Grayslake, on the outer edges of the Chicago suburbs, and also the fact that I had lived in northern Illinois for several years before returning to my home state of Wisconsin.

After clearing it with the staff, Sadie and I met Burt and the photographer at TOPS, where they took numerous photos and got to observe Sadie's therapy in action as she received cranial-sacral massage and worked out on the Hydro-Treadmill. The interview with Burt lasted well over an hour and seemed to go very well, but as with the article in the *Waukesha Freeman* three months earlier, we waited on pins and needles for several weeks to see how it turned out.

Negative media coverage, we knew, would be worse than no coverage at all and could actually set back Sadie's cause significantly. We realized that not everyone understood or approved of putting so many resources into saving one disabled dog when there were so many people in need, and we had to always be prepared to handle any negative back-lash.

And then at last the article appeared! Sunday, August 19, 2012, we had front-page coverage yet again, with Burt's column in the lower right-hand corner of the cover of the *Daily Herald*. Beneath the byline Burt Constable's Suburban Stories was the headline, AFTER SHE WAS SHOT IN HEAD, SADIE'S NOW RELEARNING TO WALK. And below the headline was a cute photo of Sadie sitting in the grass and "smiling," with a yellow bandanna knotted around her neck.

My eye jumped down farther and I saw that the article itself got right to the point: *The only thing veterinarians know for certain is that shortly after giving birth to her litter of puppies, the lovable mutt known as Sadie was shot in the head . . .*

As I read onward, my excitement grew. The article did a terrific job of relating Sadie's backstory, how she and I met, her ongoing treatment and therapy, and her hopes and prospects for the future.

"Sadie, you're an absolute star," I told her as I carefully refolded the paper and smoothed out any creases, saving it for Sadie's burgeoning scrapbook that was now bursting at the seams with photographs, notes, articles, printouts, and clippings.

Sure enough, we saw a bump in donations and online traffic after the *Daily Herald* article ran. By now Sadie's presence was global, and she was receiving messages and support from places as far away as Russia, China, Ireland, Switzerland, Canada, Norway, England, France, and Australia, in addition to her fans and supporters in almost all fifty states.

* * *

Labor Day weekend 2012 offered the perfect opportunity to sit back, relax for a few days, reflect on the incredible summer we'd just had, and refocus our energies for the remainder of the year. As of Sunday, September 2, 289 people had donated a total of $7,300 to Saving Sadie via our ChipIn account, while many more had contributed via checks to the credit union.

Originally we had earmarked those donations for surgery to have Sadie's leg amputated, back when we thought that would be part of her rehab plan, but once that option was off the table, we refocused our fund-raising on supporting Sadie's ongoing care. Fortunately, Sadie's friends and contributors totally supported that decision. Like all of us on Team Sadie, they only wanted what was best for her.

I thought it was important to take some time over that weekend, during a rare and precious quiet moment, to sit down on the floor in the living room with Sadie at my side, surrounded by brown paper grocery bags full of the hundreds of letters of support and encouragement that people had sent. I held Sadie's head in my lap, resting her chin on my knee and stroking her velvety ears as I read the messages to her aloud. Sparky stretched out along my other side as Kit Kat and Miss Kitty observed from a distance, perched on either arm of the couch, paws folded serenely beneath them as they gazed on us and blinked sleepily.

None of us really knows how much dogs truly comprehend of human speech; perhaps nothing more than a handful of trained commands. (Even though they give us those sweet, innocent looks with their cocked heads and expressive faces, when we just know they are only pretending not to understand what we're saying.)

I believe with all my heart that dogs can sense, experience, and interpret emotion, intuiting and responding to their person's feelings in a form of communication that goes far deeper than anything mere language can ever touch; when it comes to dogs, it is truly possible to talk without ever uttering a single word.

Sadie's supporters, these people whose names we'd never heard before and whose faces we'd never seen, had taken the time and energy and effort to write to Sadie. They deserved to have her hear their words, regardless of how much of the content Sadie understood. So I randomly grabbed a note from the top of the pile, opened it, and started reading aloud. "This one is from Ann in California," I explained to Sadie. "It says, 'You can do it, girl.'"

"'Sadie, you are so brave.' From Megan in the UK."

"'Give Sadie a big kiss for me and tell her I love her, and I will pray every night for her, always.' That's from Brooke."

"Your 'adopted Aunt Linda' writes, 'Please give Sadie hugs and kisses for me.'"

I wanted to keep reading, but I couldn't see through the tears filling my eyes. The love, care, and affection for Sadie that I could feel in these simple yet heartfelt words were overwhelming.

"What a miracle you are, Sadie," I whispered to her, staring down into her deep amber eyes. "And to think, just a little over four months ago you were considered a throwaway dog, a piece of living, breathing garbage, with nothing to offer the world, doomed to spend the rest of your life locked in a metal cage at a shelter, just waiting to die. And look at you now! If only more people could see you and understand the power of what love and faith and hope can make happen in the world."

Sadie wagged her tail, seeming to understand. I pulled her into my lap and wrapped my arms around her, hugging her tight. I let her stay up well past her ten p.m. bedtime that night, reading note after note full of tender hope, fervent wishes, and endless good cheer. "Sadie, you are loved," I told her simply as I finally kissed her forehead and tucked her into her bed. "You are nothing but loved in this world."

The next day we were back to therapy as usual, Power Plate before breakfast, swimming, peanut ball, massage, and a few new exercises I had invented, too. But when I made her work for food to go up the stairs, something changed. On the second-to-the-top step, after much cajoling from me, Sadie raised herself from a sitting position and went up the final step all on her own! I still held out my arms to make sure she didn't fall, but she had clearly taken the final step under her own power. "You did it, Sadie, you did it!" I walloped in joy. She seemed a little startled by my outburst, but I stroked her and ruffled her fur to let her know it was okay. "You are my amazing girl!"

I had always referred to her weak, shaky back legs as "noodles." I guessed that now those wiggly noodles were firming up and becoming "al dente"! I couldn't wait to share this amazing news with all of Sadie's fans and followers in my Labor Day newsletter that I posted on our website the next day.

After giving a recap of Sadie's exciting breakthrough, I ended with, "For all of your encouragement, I say THANK

YOU to each and every one of you! YOU are the people who made this happen! Thank you for all of your kind words, funding, and love that made this very special moment possible!"

I was truly humbled by the support we were receiving, and realized that all my years of fiercely proud independence had prevented me from truly understanding what teamwork was all about. "It takes a village," indeed. This was just another of Sadie's remarkable gifts to me, during this time when I was "supposedly" saving her. Clearly, the reverse was true, and she had led me to a higher purpose, lifting me up from the somewhat mundane and predictable life I hadn't even realized I was living before she came into my world. One helpless, hopeless little dog had truly blessed me beyond anything I could ever have imagined.

Ever since I had met Lisa and Noah, the young man injured in Iraq, at Jammin' on Janesville in July, I had been meaning to visit Acres of Hope and Aspirations, the nearby rehab facility that Lisa owned and where Noah and many other brain-damaged people worked to relearn and regain the basic life skills they had lost due to traumatic brain injury. Finally, in early September, the perfect opportunity presented itself when I was invited to a silent auction and fund-raising event there, where the special guest speaker would be the nationally known stand-up comedian Dobie Maxwell.

As soon as I entered the grounds of Acres of Hope and Aspirations, I knew I was someplace special, a place where magic happened every day. Set on nearly five acres of dense, rural, beautifully rugged woodland, the complex included a rehab center, a log cabin, and a small working farm, along with relaxing gardens, a large pond with a fountain, and glorious waterfalls.

Lisa, a registered nurse, had started the center in 2010 after years of working with brain-injured people and witnessing firsthand the toll these injuries took on people's lives, personally, professionally, financially, and emotionally. She was committed to creating a warm, nurturing, supportive environment—completely opposite to the cold, clinical, sterile environment of most hospitals and rehab centers—where the beauty of nature and the love of animals could play a major role in the healing process. Care at Acres of Hope and Aspirations was available as day treatment, respite care, or short- and long-term rehabilitation, and all care was provided by RNs, CNAs, and certified rehab case managers.

Acres of Hope and Aspirations' two mottos were *Where Healing Is Nurtured by Nature*, and *Where Ordinary Rehab Is Transformed into the Extra-Ordinary.* I thought to myself, *The mottos are certainly appropriate—this place IS extra-ordinary.* I wandered the grounds, feeling the first chill of autumn in the air and noticing the first edges of orange, red, and goldenrod in the leaves of the majestic oak and maple trees. Everywhere I turned I was struck by the understated grace and beauty of the place—the solemn, therapeutic gardens, colorful eruptions of wildflowers, and narrow, winding, muddy paths that led deep into the forest's dark and shadowy heart.

As beautiful as the setting was, though, it was the numerous animals that delighted my eye and stirred my soul, all uncaged, unrestrained, and wandering the grounds freely—pet deer, a miniature donkey, ponies, duck, geese, chickens, tortoises, peacocks, cats, and rabbits. The animals were part of "Creatures of Rehab," a program of animal-assisted therapy that Acres of Hope and Aspirations offered its patients.

By helping care for the animals, the brain-injured patients enhanced their cognitive skills and self-esteem while simultaneously receiving the love, support, and nurturing that the animals provided. Some of the animals were even disabled themselves, including Queenie, a blind Shetland pony who gave rides to children while being led around the grounds by her seeing-eye guide, an enormous potbellied pig named Batman, and Kisses, a miniature donkey who limped due to a disabled hoof.

My heart was touched so deeply by what I was seeing, and the possibilities that were unfolding right in front of me. Magic. It was absolute magic, pure and simple. *These animals, just like Sadie, have a special role to play. They can be inspiring, they can be symbolic, they can represent hope. Their very presence can be therapeutic. They can touch people on a deeper level, reaching inside to a place beyond words, especially for adults and children with special needs, who may not be able to communicate verbally or in traditional ways. These animals can help people heal their broken bodies, repair their damaged brains, and soothe their troubled souls. This is all part of Sadie's mission. I need to find a way to make it happen. I need to do this—I have received a calling, and it is my life's work now.*

* * *

Later, when Dobie Maxwell, the comedian performing that night, came onstage to do his show, he was amazing! A Milwaukee native now based in Chicago, he toured nationally with his stand-up routine, having appeared with famous comics such as Jay Leno, Jerry Seinfeld, Chris Rock, and Tim Allen, to name a few. It was his love for, and commitment to, animals that brought him to this fund-raising event in little old Muskego, and I had an inkling that he could become a valuable addition to Team Sadie. I just had to get up the courage to ask him.

When he finished his set and came offstage, I swallowed hard and approached him nervously. I asked if he'd like to learn more about Sadie and then handed him one of Sadie's business cards. Dobie, a tall, gregarious guy with slicked-back brown hair and a big, booming voice and an even bigger smile, immediately put me at ease with his warmth and kindness, banishing my nerves.

As we talked he was very interested in Sadie, and even suggested Sadie and I join him as guests on *The Mothership Connection*, the Sunday-night talk show he hosted on WLIP, an AM radio station in Kenosha. (I later learned that Dobie had been involved in a near-fatal car accident in 1993. He was badly injured and it took him six months to learn to walk again—no doubt he was relating to Sadie's saga on a deeply personal level.)

Dobie suggested I be a guest on his show along with his friend Asia Voight. Asia Voight! Of course I knew of her, the famous intuitive guide and animal communicator. It would be an incredible opportunity to have Asia do a reading with Sadie and help me understand what Sadie was thinking and feeling about all she had gone through and the things we were doing now to rehab her. Dobie and I exchanged contact info and he promised to call me in a few weeks to schedule the radio show with me and Sadie and Asia.

As I drove home that evening, excited to tell Sadie all about my amazing day, I thought about all the incredible people I was meeting: brave Noah and his struggle to walk and talk again after a horrific injury; Lisa, a devoted nurse who'd built a sanctuary of hope, healing, and second chances in the leafy Wisconsin woods; Dobie Maxwell, the warm-hearted comic with the razor-sharp wit and the broad, generous soul; and now Asia Voight, world-famous inspirational speaker and medium.

All this is because of Sadie, I thought in amazement as I pulled into my driveway and doused the headlights. *None of these people would have come into my life without her. This is Sadie, working her life-altering magic on me yet again.*

CHAPTER EIGHT

The Mothership
Connection

The autumn and winter of 2012 was a busy time for Sadie and me, full of several significant milestones. She continued to make progress in her rehab, slowly but steadily. Her legs had strengthened and improved so much that she was now placing the bottoms of her paws on the ground to walk, maybe not every time, but most of the time. This meant that the chronic abrasion she'd had on her back left leg from dragging it had healed so much that I no longer needed to cover it with a vet wrap.

We were still working on her stair exercises, and her "al dente" back legs were more stable now and had started reaching for the next step, which was a huge improvement. By the second of November, she was able to do one full step on her own, without my help. I truly felt that we were on the verge of a major breakthrough and that Sadie would be walking again very, very soon. I was confident that all the toil, sweat, and tears of the past six months were about to blossom into something wonderful.

The most extraordinary thing that happened during this time was that Sadie got out of diapers at last! The vets (other than Dr. Jodie) who'd first seen Sadie projected that, because of her spinal injuries, she'd be urinary and fecally incontinent for the rest of her life. But Sadie proved them wrong, wrong, wrong! She had been gradually gaining better control over her bodily functions, and so I had been able to keep her out of diapers for longer and longer periods of time during the day. It was mostly at night when she'd have problems, or first thing in the morning, when her bladder was too full for her to go on her own and I had to help her empty it.

Dr. Laurie from TOPS had recommended a homeopathic remedy for dogs with urinary incontinence called Leaks No More, and that had helped greatly. Now Sadie was staying dry all night and then rushing down the stairs by herself in the morning when she needed to go. I would let her outside and she would urinate without any help! She had been detoxing on her own almost since the beginning, so now she had achieved true independence in the "bathroom department."

I think my constantly reinforcing the command of "go potty, go potty" had helped Sadie make the connection, along with watching Sparky "go potty," too. I was so proud of what Sadie had accomplished! Not to mention how much easier it made my life, no longer having to diaper a nearly fifty-pound dog several times a day.

Meanwhile, in addition to all our at-home efforts, Sadie was now back to swimming several times a week at Think Pawsitive while also still getting intensive treatment at Dr. Jodie's and at TOPS. Originally we had thought Sadie would only need to go to TOPS until the end of October, but she was doing so well, and making so much progress, that we decided to continue her treatments there for at least the rest of the year.

For all the fantastic physical progress Sadie was making, I noticed the biggest improvements in her mental and emotional state. There was no longer any trace of the blank, empty-eyed, detached Sadie I had seen at the shelter and in our first days together. She was now a bright, energetic, curious dog who loved people and loved life and never complained about her limitations. She adored trips in the car, when she could sit up tall and straight and press her nose firmly against the window, watching everything that flew by in a state of delighted wonder.

Sadie savored every little detail in life, from the smell of fresh-cut grass to a sticky hug and sloppy ice cream kiss from a toddler to a dish of raw food placed in front of her. I had had dogs all my life, but I had never seen a dog eat the way Sadie did. Most dogs bolt their food like crazed lunatics whose lives depend on devouring the entire meal in under twelve seconds, but Sadie actually took her time to smell and taste and thoroughly chew every little morsel, reveling in the pleasure it gave her.

I often felt that Sadie understood the fate she had been saved from, and having that awareness allowed her to appreciate life so much more than most humans do. Animals, especially animals like Sadie, have so much to teach us about our own lives, if we would only listen.

Gearing up for the holidays was especially fun with Sadie around. There were so many people to reach out to and thank for all their support during the year. I decided a good way to do this was through a mass Christmas card mailing. I didn't have the budget to hire a professional photographer and designer, so I plopped a Santa stocking cap on Sadie's head, gave her a teddy bear, and posed her beneath the Christmas tree in the front lobby of Dr. Jodie's clinic, then took a photo. I used that photo on the front of the card along with the phrase, "Don't Stop Believing," and then inside I put a reproduction of Sadie's paw print with the message, "Greeting you with my paws extended for this holiday season and all year long. Love, Sadie."

Together Sadie and I signed, addressed, and mailed over 250 cards to friends, family, and Sadie supporters worldwide. I wished we could do more and thank every person individually, especially all the people who had donated money toward her care, but for now, this would have to do. "Next year," I promised her, "we'll find a way to do even more to thank your friends and fans." In my mind I was thinking, *Next year we'll be sending out a Christmas card that shows Sadie standing up and walking.* What holiday gift could be better than that?

Dobie Maxwell, the comedian I'd met in September at Acres of Hope and Aspirations, made good on his promise to keep in touch and have Sadie and me as guests on his program along with famed animal communicator Asia Voight. Our first appearance was scheduled for Sunday, December 16, but Sadie and I actually made our first radio appearance a week earlier, on a different station, WKLH, a classic rock FM station in Milwaukee.

That appearance came about when my friend Chris and I attended a fund-raiser at a local concert venue a few weeks earlier, for a police officer who'd been severely injured on his way home from work when he was struck by a wrong-way drunk driver on the expressway. At that fund-raising event WKLH was auctioning off a Sunday-night spot on their popular program, *Hey Mom, I'm on WKLH*, and Chris and I were the winning bidders!

So on Sunday, December 9, Chris, Sadie, and I took our places behind the microphone with the host for the six-to-seven-p.m. show. I was a little nervous, this being my first time on the radio, but I so appreciated the opportunity to share Sadie's story with an increasingly wide audience. We had been determined to extend our media outreach beyond newspapers and the Internet, and now here we were, establishing a presence on the radio, too.

Part of the fun of being guests on the program was getting to choose my own playlist of songs from the many thousands in WKLH's library. I didn't want to just choose random songs, or songs that were necessarily personal favorites; I wanted to somehow honor Sadie with my choices, even if only indirectly.

After much thought, I settled on Journey's "Don't Stop Believin'," Bruce Springsteen's "Born to Run," Joni Mitchell's "Help Me," "O-o-h Child" by the Five Stairsteps (for the line "things are gonna get easier . . ."), "Imagine" by John Lennon, and a handful of others. Chris was initially horrified when I told her I wanted to use "Legs" by ZZ Top, because of the line, "She's got legs, she knows how to use them," in reference to Sadie.

"Joal! You can't use that—it's horrible," Chris complained.

"Why not?" I replied. "Sadie's story is not all doom and gloom. Sadie has a sense of humor—she likes to make people laugh. I actually sing this song to her all the time and she thinks it's hilarious. So why not play it on the radio?"

Having convinced Chris, I added ZZ Top's "Legs" to my playlist. Between playing the songs and sharing Sadie's story with listeners all over Southeast Wisconsin, the hour passed quickly and in no time, it was over. Sadie had been so perfectly well behaved in the studio, greeting everyone like a pro and sitting quietly at my feet while we were on the air, I had no qualms about pursuing future radio and even TV appearances for her. Clearly, Sadie was a media darling in the making.

After WKLH we were excited, gearing up for our next radio show, scheduled for the following Sunday on WLIP AM 1050 with Dobie Maxwell, when the unimaginable happened. On December 14, a deeply troubled young man named Adam Lanza walked into Sandy Hook Elementary School in Newtown, Connecticut, and murdered twenty children and six adults in cold blood. Like the rest of America and the rest of the world, I was shocked and horrified beyond belief as I watched the news unfold.

As a mother and grandmother myself, I couldn't begin to imagine the anguish and grief of those families, to lose those sweet, precious little lives in such a violent and brutal way. I wondered, too, about the killer, about what could make someone so young act out with such rage, hatred, and hopelessness. I knew there were a lot of adolescents like Adam out there, even if most of them didn't express themselves through such extreme measures.

It was said that Adam, like many young men who commit mass murder, had been teased and bullied in school. "Kids need to feel welcomed and embraced, whatever their challenges and differences," I said to myself. "They need to hear and learn the message that being different is okay. Sadie, in overcoming her challenges, can be an example of that; she can teach people, especially kids, how to embrace differences. That's an essential part of her story."

I believe that was the first moment I realized that Sadie and I would eventually take up the banner of the anti-bullying movement, but I just wasn't sure yet exactly how to make that happen. Even with all of Sadie's remarkable progress and improvement, her care was still essentially a full-time job, and given my other "real" full-time job, I couldn't yet see how we could take on even more challenges and add more commitments to the mix. For the moment I just needed to be patient and have faith—everything would happen, in its own time.

We were still reeling following the news from Newtown, and our hearts were still heavy with grief two days later, on Sunday, December 16, when Chris, Sadie, and I drove to Kenosha to appear on Dobie's show, *The Mothership Connection*. The show tended to highlight subjects with a paranormal theme (hence the name), but since it was Dobie's show, he was free to book guests on a wide range of topics, and given his support of animal issues, Sadie was a natural fit.

Unfortunately, Asia was not able to join us for the show that night, but Dobie promised that he'd get us all together on the show sometime in the future. We could have chosen to do the show remotely, via telephone, but Chris and I (and Sadie!) decided to drive to the studio in Kenosha to appear in person, so Dobie and everyone else could meet Sadie and she could work her magic on them, just as she had on all the folks at WKLH.

Dobie's show was a blast! Again the hour passed so

quickly, and we found that Dobie is a real showman, a natural entertainer, and a genuinely nice man who was so kind, warm, and funny, allowing us to tell Sadie's story and really connect with his audience of devoted listeners.

The news got even better two days later, when Dobie featured Sadie in his "Dobie Maxwell's 'Dented Can' Diary," a blog/column he regularly wrote for onmilwaukee.com, Milwaukee's biggest and best known online digital magazine. The blog post was titled, "Sadie Steals the Show," and after providing a bit of Sadie's backstory, Dobie wrote, *Sadie was pure magic and made everyone feel great. She has a very tangible vibe that radiates from her at all times, and she was the undisputed star of the evening from the instant she got out of the car and limped up to the door of the radio station.*

"Sadie!" I shouted to her as I read the computer screen in my study. "Dobie says you were the 'undisputed star of the evening!' " She smiled and wagged her tail. I continued reading in earnest.

Seeing her in person and feeling her wonderful energy was one of the most inspiring moments I think I've ever had, Dobie's article continued. *She will be an inspiration to all who see her.* Normally I would have squealed with delight at reading those words, but my throat was too clogged with tears for me to even utter a sound.

What a beautiful article, and a beautiful tribute. I spent so much time with Sadie on a daily basis, twenty-four/seven when I wasn't at work, that I sometimes felt I had developed a type of tunnel vision where she was concerned. Of course to me Sadie was beautiful and wonderful and remarkable and inspirational, but I was her mom and I loved her, so my opinion was not exactly objective. Maybe other people saw her as just an ordinary dog, or worse, as a disabled dog with a multitude of special needs, a dog who sucked up lots of valuable resources and had nothing meaningful to offer in return.

But when I read an article like Dobie's, or saw some of the hope-filled and inspiring messages posted on Sadie's Facebook page, or watched the way Sadie interacted with special needs people like Noah from Acres of Hope and Aspirations, all my doubts and fears and reservations disappeared. Other people *were* able to feel and experience and be moved by Sadie's magic; they only had to be willing to open their eyes and their hearts wide enough to do so.

When Christmas 2012 arrived I was fortunate to be able to spend the day enjoying a fantastic Christmas Day brunch with my extended family—daughters, sons-in-law, grandchildren—at my older daughter Joey's home, celebrating as we always did, with a formal brunch in our pj's, drinking mimosas and coffee and opening presents under a gigantic tree. Joey is a natural-born hostess, and she knew just the right touches to make it an extra-special event.

It was wonderful to share quality time with my family when we all had such busy lives, but there was some discomfort in the air as well. We didn't talk much about Sadie, but I got the sense that my daughters were still coming to terms with Sadie and the way she had completely taken over my life. I was sorry for the tension it was causing, but I truly believed that ultimately they would see that all the effort on Sadie's behalf would be worth it in the end. Until then, we were all slightly walking on eggshells around one another, and that caused me deep sadness and concern.

One of the highlights of my Christmas was spending quiet time at home with Sadie, Sparky, Kit Kat, and Miss Kitty. My special gift to Sadie was a sled, just a kids' plastic sled from Target. The wonderful Beth, a local law enforcement officer, had sewn a custom-made cushioned fabric insert for the sled with an attached blanket that featured Sadie's paw print in green (her signature color). The insert had shiny red ribbons on the edges so it could be tied down and secured inside the sled, thereby keeping Sadie warm and protecting her from all the bumps and other rough spots in the snow.

On the day after Christmas I took Sadie to a local dog park, where I let her try out the sled for the very first time. The weather was perfect for sledding, with bright, unfiltered sunshine filling the sky and temperatures just above freezing. The air was crisp and quiet, all harsh sounds muffled, right angles softened, and sharp edges blunted by a fresh, downy shroud of snow. The trees in the distance were shorn of all leaves but still managed to look elegant, their branches encased in lacy gloves and frozen sleeves of ice.

As I pulled Sadie in her brand-new sled up the gently rolling hills packed hard with snow, the air was fresh with notes of evergreen and peppermint, and my breath came fast as I stomped through the rutted tracks and frozen impressions of heavy-soled boots. Initially I thought Sadie might be scared of sledding, but she absolutely loved it! She took to the sled like it was made for her, sitting up tall and proud as I pulled her to the top of a hill and gave her a determined push.

I laughed so hard when the sled hurtled down the hill like a bowling ball and people scattered like pins to get out of her way! I ran down to the bottom of the hill and as soon as I got there, Sadie refused to get out of the sled and instead begged me to take her back to the top again.

This dog park was a kind of hidden gem, located in the Milwaukee suburbs on the county grounds, where for years an old sanitarium stood, a looming, shadowy, dark-windowed relic of the Victorian age, a time not so different from ours, when people with diseases and differences were shunned, shamed, and marginalized, left to wither in institutions until they died, conveniently out of sight and out of mind. *Just like what would have happened to Sadie, had fate not intervened*, I thought with a shudder.

After a few trips down the hill, I guided the sled to flat land and after pulling Sadie for a short distance to introduce her to the feeling, I took off at a run, sprinting across the open field, building up speed so she could feel the breeze parting her fur and the wind buffeting her face.

Sadie absolutely loved riding fast on the sled. Her tongue wagged, her eyes glowed, and her whole body seemed to vibrate with life, energy, and excitement. I had never before seen her so fully engaged, so fully immersed, in anything.

Then I realized that Sadie must love this feeling so much because it reminded her what it felt like to run. She wasn't born this way, hobbled, hopping, and reduced to dragging herself across the floor. I had only known her in this diminished state, but she had had an entire life before I met her, a life where she was tall and straight and strong, a muscular hunting dog with powerful legs that propelled her forward, from a slow trot to a loping gallop to a flat-out run, racing through the rough Appalachian hills of her home, sniffing out pheasants and badgers and fleet-footed hare. That memory still lived somewhere deep inside her, like a dormant muscle just begging to be exercised, a tiny flame always flickering, waiting for someone to throw open the doors and let oxygen rush in, whipping that nascent flame back to full, glorious, blazing life.

We were both exhausted, invigorated but also spent, as I pulled her in the sled back to the parking lot and popped open the hatch on my SUV. I lifted Sadie from the sled and placed her inside, then I jumped in and sat beside her with my legs dangling over the edge, knocking snow from my boots and rubbing my mittened hands for warmth. Our breath was visible, clouds wreathing our mouths as we watched the sun dip, tipping toward its early, post-solstice descent into darkness.

I wrapped my arms around Sadie's shoulders and cuddled her for warmth. "Thank you, Sadie," I whispered against her ear, "for making 2012 one of the best years of my life. You have taught me so much, inspired me to dream bigger, to try so many new and different things. In exchange I promise to make your 2013 amazing, and to make it the year you *will* walk again."

CHAPTER NINE
Sadie Goes to Asia

The year 2013 began with a bang, and a full slate of Sadie meet-and-greets, now taking place every two weeks at various Pet Worlds around southeastern Wisconsin, along with other personal appearances, interviews, and media bookings. We scored a major coup with our first TV interview and profile on *Today's TMJ4*, Milwaukee's local NBC affiliate. This was a huge step forward in our plan to expand media coverage of Sadie beyond print and Internet to radio, television, and more.

Today's TMJ4 reporter Stephanie Graham met us on January 9 at the Pet World in Menomonee Falls, during one of Sadie's regular meet-and-greets with customers, staff, and the general public. With us was Jessica, the massage therapist for humans who had been giving Sadie massage as part of her ongoing therapy.

Stephanie and her cameraman spent a long time filming Sadie in action, from her being massaged by Jessica and demonstrating her attempts at walking to being wheeled in a shopping cart and interacting with kids. Stephanie also interviewed me on camera, asking about how I found Sadie, the logistics of her care, how she had changed my life, and so forth. Afterward I felt the interview had gone really well, but as always we couldn't know how the final product turned out until we actually saw the segment on TV, and as always we worried a little bit about negative media coverage and the impact something like that would have on Saving Sadie.

It was a bit of a wait, but on January 22, the story was finally broadcast! I was curled up in bed in my flannel pj's, anxiously clutching the remote and with all the animals huddled around me for warmth as our segment began. We had scored the all-important Special Assignment spot on the ten p.m. newscast. "Okay, guys, this is it!" I said, turning up the volume.

Longtime Channel 4 anchorman Mike Jacobs, looking distinguished in his dark blazer and colorfully striped tie, introduces the piece. "A Muskego woman has made it her mission to save a dog that nobody wanted," he begins.

Muskego woman—that's me!

Co-anchor Carole Meekins continues, "Susan Kim has an inspiring story of perseverance." The camera cuts to reporter Susan in the studio, positioned in front of a wide screen with SAVING SADIE in large block letters among a collage of Sadie photos. "What started as a tragedy is now a blessing for a Muskego woman and her special dog," Susan reports. The scene moves to Pet World, with Sadie relaxing on a Turkish carpet as Jessica gives her a luxurious, head-to-tail, deep-muscle massage.

"Sadie! There you are!" I squealed, pointing the remote at the screen. "Look at you, Boo-boo!" I was dazzled by how telegenic Sadie was. She truly looked amazing on film, with her glossy black fur and warm brown markings clear and vividly defined. She gazed straight into the camera as her amber eyes lit up and her face glowed, intelligent and expressive.

"For Sadie, I have to be careful when working the neck

muscles," Jessica explains. "There's some extra straining going on there, just because she can't use those hind legs."

Now cut to me with Sadie in a shopping cart. "Believe me, this was not on my bucket list, to rehab a paralyzed dog," I say, stroking her head. "It just wasn't. However, she's just very thankful, and that's what makes it all worthwhile."

Despite her challenges, you can tell this persevering pooch is very happy, and loving her second chance at life, Susan explains in voiceover.

"She's just taught me so much," I add, rubbing Sadie's shoulders as she sits up in the shopping cart looking absolutely adorable. "She just will not sit down in the car because she's absorbing all the traffic and everything that life has to offer. She has taught me we have to love not only animals and people, no matter what kind of baggage they have, and I think it's absolutely huge, because we *all* have baggage."

Back to the anchors in the studio. Carole Meekins says with an admiring smile, "Well, Sadie does have some guardian angels."

Mike Jacobs readily concurs. "It's like that look on Sadie's face almost says thank you," he marvels.

I lowered the volume, leaned back against my pillows, and pulled Sadie close, wrapping her in my arms. "You are a natural, Sadie, no doubt about it," I said, stroking her head. "The camera loves you, and you are a star." I was humbled to think how many thousands, probably tens of thousands, of viewers in southeast Wisconsin had seen Sadie's story and been touched by what they had seen. "You are on the way," I told her. "Pretty soon everybody will know your name."

Following Sadie's appearance on *Today's TMJ4*, we had another TV appearance a month later. In early February we were interviewed by Maximilian Hess, a student at Marquette University in Milwaukee, for a feature story on MUTV, Marquette University Television News. I didn't mind that this story was only running on a student television station; it was great practice for Sadie and me to improve our interview skills while also spreading Sadie's message to a new and untapped audience.

Max, a bright, eager young man with clipped brown hair and glasses, came to the house to interview us, which gave him and his cameraman the chance to see Sadie in action and film it for the report: Sadie playing with her toys, going upstairs (with help), flying downstairs (with no help), playing peek-a-boo with a blanket thrown over her head, and frolicking in the thick layer of freshly fallen snow that blanketed the woods surrounding my house. I appreciated the deep interest that Max showed in Sadie and how much time he devoted to getting to know her and learning more about her life.

When the feature was broadcast on February 20, the segment opened with a shot of Sadie sitting in the snow, paws folded regally beneath her as she gazed at the camera with an intense, serious expression on her face. *This is Sadie*, Max's voiceover began. *She's not your usual dog. In fact, she's everything but that. Her owner, Joal, lives in a quaint house in Muskego and has a true heart for animals . . .*

When the two-minute-nineteen-second segment finished, I sat back in awe, moved by the beauty of the piece and by how Sadie had been given the opportunity to shine on screen yet again. *There's so much bad news in the world, so many evil people*, I thought. *And at the same time, there are also so many worthy causes that deserve focus and attention. And yet people are willing to give airtime to Sadie, to share her story and help generate support. If not for Sadie, I would never have realized how truly kind and generous people can be.*

In the midst of so many wonderful things happening, especially in terms of raising Sadie's profile among the media, we faced some challenges and setbacks as well. At the end of January, I had to ask Marnette to cut back on her work with Saving Sadie in order to bring someone on board who was able to devote more hours to the tasks, especially Internet and social media-related tasks, that were becoming more and more complex and time-consuming.

This was painful and difficult for both of us; Marnette had put her heart and soul into Saving Sadie right from the beginning. We never could have accomplished what we'd accomplished without her incredible effort and her valuable connections. But because she lived hundreds of miles away and had so many commitments in addition to Saving Sadie, I knew our needs would soon outdistance what she was able to provide.

In truth, I worried about Marnette. She had a full-time job, did lots of pet sitting for friends, was mom to a houseful of cats of her own, and put in countless hours volunteering with pet rescue organizations in South Carolina. If there was a way to lighten her load when it came to Saving Sadie, I knew that was the right thing to do.

Happily, my friend Dave Johnson put me in touch with Valerie Alba, a local woman who was running her own business as a virtual assistant. I went to interview Valerie and we clicked right away. I was impressed with her knowledge, skills, and enthusiasm, especially in the complex and quickly changing world of social media. I hired her immediately and since then Valerie has been in charge of managing Sadie's social media presence, which includes her website, email newsletter, Facebook fan page, Twitter, Instagram, Pinterest, and so much more. Today Valerie remains a vital member of Team Sadie, helping us stay in touch with friends and supporters around the world while disseminating Sadie's message far and wide.

In the midst of everything else going on, Sadie's therapy also continued in earnest as we pressed harder and harder, always fine-tuning her treatments and therapies, still searching for that elusive "magic answer" that would get her walking again. At the end of January, we began a new type of hydro treadmill therapy with Dr. Kristin Luginbill at Lakeshore Veterinary Specialists in Glendale, a suburb of Milwaukee. This was different from the hydro treadmill that Sadie used as part of her therapy at TOPS.

For this hydro treadmill, visualize, if you will, a treadmill surrounded by a clear glass box. Dr. Luginbill, a tall, outgoing, warmhearted woman clad in hip waders with her long blond hair secured in a ponytail, climbs into the box and places Sadie on the treadmill, straddling Sadie between her legs and holding up Sadie's back end. Once the box is closed and secured it slowly fills with water until the water covers Sadie's legs and she's able to take steps on the treadmill with her front paws while Dr. Luginbill moves Sadie's back legs, trying to train her legs to move in an alternating rhythm, right-left, right-left, right-left, known as "patterning," re-creating the pattern of steps that constitute a dog's normal gait. While Dr. Luginbill and Sadie were in the glass pool, I would be standing outside the box in front of Sadie, encouraging her to keep taking steps.

This therapy was intense and grueling for me, for Dr. Luginbill, and for Sadie, but we believed it offered Sadie the best opportunity to walk again, so we were committed to sticking with it, long term. "Whatever it takes, Sadie," I would tell her after each of these exhausting sessions, as I dried her damp fur in a big fluffy towel and felt the fatigue radiating from her muscles. "This is the year that you *will* walk again."

Developing a relationship with an animal, whether a dog, cat, horse, or other creature, is a lot like developing a relationship with a human being. The more time you spend together, the closer you become; the more you begin to understand the other's thoughts, fears, hopes, and dreams, and the more you can feel what each other is feeling. It is as if you share a single mind, heart, and soul, and can access the other's thoughts and emotions, even learning to anticipate how the other will react in certain situations.

Certainly Sadie and I had developed an especially close physical and emotional bond in the nine months since I had adopted her, and yet I still had many unanswered questions. I knew without a doubt that Sadie loved me; she showed me that every single day. My questions centered more around Sadie's past, her memories, good and bad, and how she coped with processing the trauma she had endured. I so wished she could tell me about what had happened to her in those harsh Appalachian hills, even though I knew that hearing the whole story would undoubtedly break my heart.

I often suspected that Sadie may have been shot by a man wearing a hat. Sadie loved everyone; to her every stranger was simply a friend she hadn't met yet. The only time she ever reacted strangely and seemed upset was when she was around a man wearing a hat, especially a baseball cap. When she saw a man in a baseball cap, she would bark a fierce, angry, violent bark. This was my Sadie, a dog who never normally barked at all, so I knew she was re-acting to something that I couldn't see or understand.

It's okay, girl, don't worry, I would console her, holding her close. *Try not to think about that. The bad men are far away, and no one will ever hurt you again. I will protect you, I promise.*

I was highly intrigued by the possibility that maybe I could communicate with Sadie on a deeper level, and maybe there were people out there who could help initiate that process. In early February I got in touch with Keri Davis, a Canadian woman who practices what she calls Sacred Kinship, using her natural gifts as a medium to enable animals and their people to communicate more directly with one another.

I was especially taken by Keri's philosophy, as described on her website: "Energetically we are all one, but in our evolution as rational, thinking Beings, we have narrowed our ability to communicate with humans only." How true! Keri was committed to using her psychic gifts to reopen those channels of communication that had become closed off over time.

I felt an additional kinship with Keri when I saw that her website was dedicated to her late dog, Mukluk, who was blind and deaf and whom she described as her "beloved dog, life partner, and teacher." She wrote, "He taught me everything I DO & BE . . . I call him my little Wizard. Even though he couldn't see or hear, he lived life full out, he taught me all about energy healing, deep listening, unconditional love, and never giving up!"

Clearly, here was a woman who could understand and relate to my experiences and relationship with Sadie because she had lived something so very similar. I was excited to set up my first phone consultation with her, and when we finally spoke, I was amazed.

Keri was able to "read" Sadie almost immediately, and conveyed to me that Sadie had a great deal of light surrounding her. Sadie believed in herself, and she certainly didn't consider herself disabled. Sadie was living with a purpose, her own special purpose that drove her forward every day. Ultimately, Keri explained, Sadie's journey was more about her changing me, forcing me to open my mind and my heart, than it was about me rehabbing her, or returning her to the state of physical wholeness that she'd existed in before she was shot.

There was a very important message being conveyed here, embedded deep within Keri's words, but I wasn't quite hearing it, at least not yet. I was too focused on the surface of what she was saying, which was that Sadie was happy with the life she was living now.

"But am I doing the right thing?" I asked Keri, my voice quavering as I clutched the phone tight. "Is this what Sadie really wants?"

"Yes. Absolutely," Keri replied with a confidence that surged across the phone line and settled deep in my soul. "Sadie wants to live. She didn't want you to let her die. It wasn't her time to go. She is happy with you every single day, Joal."

I don't have words to explain what that meant to me, especially coming from an outsider, someone who had never met Sadie or seen her in person, yet who could still feel and touch and connect with her spirit on such a deep and powerful level.

"Sustain Sadie, support her, and let her be who she needs to be," Keri encouraged. "Where there is acceptance, true healing begins."

"Thank you. Thank you so much," I whispered through my tears.

I was still on a high from my conversation with Keri when Dobie Maxwell contacted me again and arranged for Sadie and me to make another appearance on his radio show, *The Mothership Connection*, at the end of March, this time with Asia Voight. I was so excited that this was finally going to happen! Asia is a superstar in the field of animal communication, and her clients swear by her ability to help them connect with their pets, both the pets they have now and those that have passed on.

The weather was terrible the night we were scheduled to be on Dobie's show, near-whiteout conditions with sleet, snow, and freezing rain, so we decided to do the program from home, calling in to the studio, rather than risk the treacherous drive to Kenosha on icy highways. Asia, who lived in Fitchburg, just outside Madison, also chose to call in rather than risk the two-hour drive to Kenosha. I worried that Asia might not be able to get a strong reading from Sadie just over the phone, but I had enough faith to trust in her highly developed spiritual gifts, not to mention the trust I had in Sadie, trust that she'd be able to project her thoughts and feelings to Asia, even from a distance.

It was just before eight o'clock on Sunday night when I settled onto the couch with a mug of hot chocolate, my fur babies surrounding me, and the phone clutched excitedly in my hand. Dobie introduced Asia first, and she described to Dobie and his listeners how she had had a near-death experience twenty-five years ago, when she was hit by a semi and trapped in her car, surrounded by flames and smoke. She had to jump out of the car to save herself but was severely burned and only given a three percent chance of survival. For three months afterward she hovered between life and death, and actually crossed over three times during that period. "Spiritual teachers were there to greet me and I heard them telepathically," she described for Dobie and his listeners.

This brush with death reawakened the dormant abilities Asia had had in her childhood that allowed her to communicate telepathically with people and with animals. "Everyone has the ability in their soul to communicate telepathically, with animals, with angels, with people who've passed," she insisted.

After a commercial break, Dobie brought me onto the program and introduced me to his audience. "Thanks for taking a ride on the Mothership," his smooth baritone voice intoned. "This is Sunday night, I'm Dobie Maxwell, Mary Marshall is here, Greg Aguirre, and we've got Asia Voight, our special guest, on the phone. Joining us now is our friend, Joal Derse Dauer. Joal, are you there?"

"I am, Dobie," I replied.

"Joal, do you want to tell Asia the story of Sadie in a nutshell?" he asked. "I know our listeners know it, but we have new listeners all the time. I just want to make sure because it's such a fascinating story, and Asia's gonna nail this, I know it, so go right ahead."

"Okay, Dobie, thanks." After clearing my throat, I related a quick summary of Sadie's backstory, about how she came into my life, the things she was doing now, and how we were working to get her walking again. I tried to keep it brief while making sure to hit the key points and especially highlight all the progress Sadie had made in the past nine months.

"I think she's adjusted to all this, but I really want to help her out," I offered. "What do *you* see, Asia?"

Asia paused, and I could hear her draw a breath before she replied in her sweet, almost childlike voice. "When you first started talking, I saw her come toward me, and actually I'm all teary-eyed over here because I just felt so much love from her, so much brilliance," she began. "Because when I first started hearing your story about this, I just spontaneously felt this anger in my heart for these people doing this, and Sadie came forward and she just said, 'No, no, don't go there, Asia. Don't be mad at those people, just remove that from your heart.'"

I sat back on my sofa, speechless. That was exactly how I

hoped, and imagined, Sadie might feel. She has such a generous spirit that it would be just like her to forgive the people who hurt and abused her.

Asia went on to describe Sadie's fighting spirit as she was perceiving it through Sadie. "Then she said, 'Don't say no to Sadie,'" Asia explained. "So what she's really saying is, she's so willing to do everything, don't even try to say no to her. She's not going to accept 'no.' That is one of the messages that she wants to spread to you, that there is nothing you can't do. She just wants to wipe the word 'no' out of people's minds when they feel limited, when they feel incapable, when they feel they're not good enough. When they feel all those blocks and limits, then she's like, 'Nu uh, we're going to do this, we're going to move forward, and we're going to do it with grace and joy and love.'"

Suddenly I was very glad that we were on the radio and not on TV, because I didn't want people to see my mouth drop open and my jaw fall to the floor. I was amazed that Asia was able to read Sadie so clearly, so strongly, from miles away and without even meeting her in person. But then it got even better.

"Sadie also said that some people, when they see her, they feel sad for her and sometimes look at you like, why would you keep her alive? Why would you do this to this dog? She said that they are in the minority but that some people still say that, and she said, 'I say to you that's not true for us, I am so glad to be here. Every day I wake up and say what's next, what can we do? What can we try?' She said that everybody, whatever kind of body they have, is in their greatest wholeness, whether you think it's limited or not, that's not the truth. It doesn't have to be the truth, and so again she says there's nothing to stop anyone; there's no reason to be stopped in your life, and she will not hear of it."

By now my goose bumps had developed goose bumps, and chills danced up and down my spine, making my whole body tingle. This was a miracle—everything I hoped and dreamed about Sadie was true.

"I feel that there are angels living in and around Sadie that have kept her alive, and that she really does embody angelic energy," Asia added in her gentle, soothing voice.

Mary Marshall, one of Dobie's co-hosts on the show, chimed in. "Can Sadie give us any information as to who hurt her?" she asked.

Asia paused, then spoke carefully. "When I first asked Sadie about these people who harmed her, she held her breath. She stopped breathing. She felt tense and started shaking her head no. She said she didn't even want to go there, she didn't want to talk about that, but she would be happy to show me images about where she used to live, what it was like, something from there."

I wasn't at all surprised that Sadie didn't want to think or communicate about the violence that nearly ended her life. Asia described how Sadie instead shared one of her favorite dreams, of a hilly place filled with pine trees, a place where she could run up and down those rocky hills, racing against the wind as she darted back and forth between the trees.

Yes, I thought, *that's the life Sadie had, before this terrible thing happened to her. That's the life I want to give back to her.*

As we continued our on-air conversation, I told Asia about Sadie's treatments and how we were constantly changing it up and adding new things. For my final question I said to Asia, "I would just like to know what else Sadie is thinking. I mean she's a happy girl, but do you have anything else, besides that she doesn't want to revisit what happened to her?"

"Yes," Asia answered emphatically. "I do want to offer you some more." She explained that she herself had been paralyzed after her accident and the doctors told her family that she would never walk again. They said that Asia would be ninety-eight percent disabled for the rest of her life.

"And I healed my paralyzed legs," she said, "and I would love to offer another session with you and Sadie when we can really go deep. I would really love to help Sadie's body, help her talk to her body, talk to her nerves, like I did, and bring in some of the angelic healers that helped me fully recover."

I was touched to the core. This was an extraordinary offer, and I couldn't wait to make it happen. As Dobie's program drew to a close, my heart and soul felt full, satisfied and at peace in a way I hadn't felt in years. Sadie and I had worked so hard, put so much time and energy and effort into fixing her body, her physical being, that I had neglected to consider her spirit, her soul. But now Sadie had spoken directly to me, she had reached me, via Asia, and forged an even stronger bond between us than ever before.

I slid off the couch and sat down on the floor beside Sadie, cradling her head in my lap. "Thank you, Boo-boo, for opening up and letting me into your world," I told her as she gazed up at me with her kind, patient, guileless amber eyes. "I apologize for having doubts, for sometimes lacking faith. Now that I know how much you want to be here, how much you appreciate everything we are doing together, I promise I will stand by your side forever; I will never, ever let you down."

CHAPTER TEN
Neurologists Deliver Sad News

I must confess that I started looking at Sadie differently during the spring of 2013. She had always been more than "just a dog" to me; I had known she was special literally from the moment our eyes first met at the shelter in Kenosha and that sad little dog hijacked my heart. My need to provide almost round-the-clock, often intimate care for her had made our connection, our bond, symbiotic and unusually strong. But after our sessions with Keri Davis and Asia Voight, I had more appreciation for Sadie's spirit, her soul, for the strong voice inside of her that longed to be set free.

It was such a relief and so reassuring to know that Sadie wanted to live, that she loved the life I was building for both of us and didn't feel hindered or depressed about her disabilities. Finally having that confidence made me more determined than ever to get her walking again and eventually fulfill her mission to inspire people, especially children, with special needs and other challenges.

In our continuing commitment to trying new things and shaking up her program, in April we added to her rehab regimen the use of air splints on Sadie's back legs. These air splints looked like a giant version of the inflatable water wings that little kids wear in the swimming pool, but these splints went from Sadie's ankles to the tops of her legs. She had this therapy two to three times a week for twenty minutes at a time. Two people had to help Sadie do this exercise once the splints were on her legs and inflated.

One person (usually me) would stand or kneel behind Sadie to stabilize her back while the other person (usually Jeff) stood in front of her, coaxing her to take forward steps using either a glob of frozen peanut butter on a large spoon, or her absolute favorite treat in the world, canned cat food. Most of the time we encouraged her with a "combo platter," alternating between the two delights.

This exercise seemed to be working! We could see that the quad muscles in Sadie's legs were getting bigger and her hamstrings were becoming stronger as a result of using the air splints. After these sessions, we usually put her on the Power Plate for a few intervals of high-speed vibration in order to increase her muscle mass and endurance and also regenerate bone.

The Power Plate was followed by some time spent relaxing on top of my bed inside the Soqi HotHouse Machine. This was a new device, a topical warming unit that I had recently added to the mix. The machine was a portable metal dome that uses far infrared rays (FIR) to gently warm the body and provide a feeling of relaxation and well-being. In addition, it was designed to stimulate blood circulation, accelerate the metabolic exchange between the body and blood vessels to relieve pain, and promote the healing process. Sadie loved spending time under the dome, growing drowsy as her whole body warmed and relaxed, at least until Miss Kitty and Kit Kat, those sneaky little heat-seekers, weaseled in to soak up any extra rays!

* * *

In March, Sadie and I had been interviewed by freelance reporter Stephanie Beecher at a friend's house, and on April 18 Stephanie's wonderful article ran on the front page of the *Wisconsin Gazette*, one of the state's largest and best-known LGBT publications, with the headline SAVING SADIE: LEFT FOR DEAD, ABUSED DOG IS REBORN THROUGH ACTS OF GENEROSITY AND HOPE, followed by a two-page spread.

The response to the article was fantastic, and we saw a large bump in web traffic and donations after the story ran. At first I was a bit surprised because Sadie and I had no direct or obvious connection to the gay and lesbian community, but the more I thought about it, the more sense it made: Sadie was an underdog, an outsider, a living being often judged by what others "thought" they knew about her just by looking. Sadie had endured and survived violence and prejudice in her life, and unfortunately so many LGBT people could relate to and connect with that experience on a deeply personal level.

Sadie's connection to the LGBT community was further solidified in June when we marched (with me pulling Sadie in her wagon) in the Pride Parade at PrideFest Milwaukee, one of the biggest LGBT festivals in the Midwest. The kindness of people was overwhelming and it seemed like just about everyone wanted to meet Sadie, talk to her, and learn more about her situation. Since attending our first PrideFest in 2013, Sadie and I have made it a point to take part in the parade every year, and we have always seen the greatest uptick in website hits, newsletter signups, and online donations in the days just after PrideFest.

*   *   *

As we approached April 24, the one-year anniversary of the day I first found Sadie and both our lives changed forever, I knew I didn't want the day to pass just like any ordinary day; I wanted it to be special and memorable. Since I had no idea when Sadie had been born, or even knew for sure how old she was, I dubbed April 24 Sadie's first "re-birthday," since it marked the day she had truly been reborn into a new life, and I decided to throw a Re-birthday/Silent Auction/Fund-raising Party in honor of this major milestone.

I wanted to mark the day in a way that would be meaningful not just for Sadie and me but also for all her friends and supporters, for all the people who had helped keep both of us afloat over this past year. Because it was going to be a big party, we needed a big venue. At first we considered holding the party at the Mitchell Park Domes, a horticultural conservatory whose three huge glass domes represent a highly visible longtime landmark on Milwaukee's south side.

When we found that staging the party at the Domes wouldn't work, we instead decided to hold the party beneath the glass atrium on the concourse at the futuristic glass-and-steel Milwaukee Intermodal Station, the city's main train and bus transportation hub on the edge of downtown. I viewed the party as a way not just to celebrate Sadie (although she was certainly worth it!) and thank all her friends and supporters, but also as a way to raise awareness and support. To that end we arranged a band for live music, games, prizes, snacks and beverages, and birthday cake (of course!) along with the silent auction.

We went all out preparing for this party, posting messages on social media and arranging advertising. A friend even helped me hire and pay to advertise the party on rotating electronic billboards above three strategic, high-traffic spots around Milwaukee. The huge billboards, done in Sadie's signature colors of yellow and green, included a close-up headshot of Sadie and proclaimed, "You're Invited—Sadie's Re-birthday Party, Sat. April 20, 11–1," with details on the location and our URL, SavingSadie.com.

When I drove past one of these billboards for the first time and saw Sadie's bright, intelligent face with her deep amber eyes staring down at me, I got chills. Here was Sadie, the paralyzed dog from the shelter, the throwaway dog no one wanted, the dog for whom euthanasia was the only "kind" option. But now her message was being broadcast to thousands of people driving past each day. In just over a year, love and hope and faith and patience had made all this happen. *And to think*, I thought, *we are only just getting started. There are so many more great things to come. There's nothing Sadie can't accomplish if she sets her mind to it.*

Things were going so well, until just a few days before the event, when disaster struck and we were told that the Intermodal Station would no longer be available to hold the Re-birthday Party. We scrambled, looking for an alternate venue, worried we'd have to cancel and leave so many people disappointed. Then, amazingly, Andy Bandy, a friend's boyfriend who owned the Lincoln Warehouse, offered to let us stage the party there.

The Lincoln Warehouse is a gigantic, five-story, 1920s-era industrial warehouse in the trendy, gentrified Third Ward neighborhood of Milwaukee that has been converted into a modern complex with offices, workshops, and studios for artists and entrepreneurs. This may not have been the ideal location for a party; for example, guests had to take a freight elevator to reach the floor where the party was held, but we were grateful to have found a place on such short notice, and Andy went all out getting the space ready for us by cleaning, painting, decorating, and bringing in and arranging tables and chairs, all so that on the day it looked absolutely fantastic.

We had to re-do all the flyers, send out mass emails announcing the change of venue, have the location changed on the electronic billboards, and paste notices on the windows at the Intermodal Station on the day of the party, hoping to alert everyone to the change. In the end more than sixty people showed up, the band was brilliant, the party lasted more than the scheduled two hours, and the silent auction raised much-needed money for Sadie's care. Sadie was the star of the event, as usual, greeting her friends and fans, sitting up in her wagon, posing for pictures, and lapping up all the attention.

For me, the best part of the whole day was when my daughter Joey arrived at the party with my granddaughter, Miranda, then aged eleven. I had invited them, of course, but I wasn't sure if they would come. There was still some tension in the family regarding my devotion to Sadie, and I knew they didn't approve of everything I was doing. So when Joey and Miranda walked in, my heart soared. The three quickly bonded as Sadie fell in love with both of them, casting her magic spell, wagging her tail, and giving them her trademark smile. As I watched the three of them interacting, I could only hope this was the beginning of warmer relations and much better things to come. *Baby steps*, I reminded myself, *baby steps. The more my family sees Sadie and the effect she has on people, the more they will welcome her into the fold. If only they could find it in their hearts to love Sadie as much as I do.*

Project Saving Sadie moved into an even more aggressive and dynamic phase that summer as we expanded her media presence and found new and exciting places to hold her meet-and-greets and other events. In May Sadie was honored to have her Saving Sadie logo placed on the back of the Muskego Police Department K9 unit's squad car. She received this honor because she had been instrumental, along with Dr. Jodie from the Animal Doctor, in helping raise funds for the police department to obtain a dog for their K9 unit.

Police dogs, as you may know, are often born and receive their early training in Europe and are then flown to their new homes around the world to receive further training, which can take several months, specific to the tasks they will be expected to perform as police dogs—for example, bomb sniffing, drug sniffing, cadaver dogs. Unsurprisingly, this whole process can be very expensive, often costing a local police department up to eighteen thousand dollars to obtain and fully train just one dog. So it was especially gratifying to help bring a dog to Muskego, and also so rewarding to witness all the new ways that we were finding for Sadie to contribute to the community, dipping her paws into more and more arenas.

* * *

In July, Sadie marked another important milestone: she started howling! From the time I had adopted her she was never much of a barker or a growler; most of our communication was through eye contact or physical connection. That was why I was so surprised the day I first heard her howl. I was driving to the bank to make a deposit and Sadie was, as usual, my attentive passenger in back, watching people and traffic and buildings flying by, when suddenly she let loose a loud, high, wailing howl, consisting of a series of jangly notes that rose and fell an octave or more before rising again to a bellowing crescendo.

Sadie! What the heck, Boo-boo! I had to be careful not to swerve into the opposite lane of traffic. A quick glance in the rearview mirror assured me that nothing was amiss; she wasn't howling out of pain or distress or as a warning. Perhaps she was responding to hearing something I couldn't hear, her sensitive ears tuning in to one of those mysterious sounds beyond the range of human perception but utterly recognizable (not to mention super exciting!) to dogs.

Once I realized that nothing was wrong, I let loose with a long, loud responding howl of my own, raising my voice until the windows of my SUV shook with the reverberations. Sadie seemed surprised but then quickly replied, matching my howl with her own, note for excruciating note.

How silly we must have looked to the people in the cars around us! I didn't care; I was just so thrilled that Sadie had finally found her voice. Clearly, she was growing stronger, bolder, prouder, and more confident with every month that passed. Little by little, piece by piece, she was rediscovering her identity as the powerful hunting dog she had once been. Sadie was finding and claiming the "real" Sadie that had been inside her all along, further proving that the people who insisted that she'd be broken forever could not have been more wrong.

Howling became a habit for Sadie and me, an in-joke only the two of us understood. She would howl at sirens and other loud noises, especially when we were driving, and I loved to egg her on, tossing off a howl and expecting her to answer me with her own bigger, louder, more garrulous call, unleashing the full throaty range of her newfound voice.

That fall we were lucky enough to connect with Charmaine Hammond, a well-known inspirational speaker from Canada, and she had Sadie and me as call-in guests on her *Think PAWsitive* radio program, giving us a fantastic opportunity to develop a new following of friends and supporters north of the border. Charmaine, who was so generous with her time, quickly became a vital member of Team Sadie, becoming a champion for Sadie's story and making Sadie part of her outreach mission.

It continued to amaze me, how many new people I met and connected with, from so many different walks of life, and all because of Sadie. She truly made my world, my whole universe, in fact, bigger every single day. I thought I had been living a pretty great life before Sadie came along; apparently, I had no idea what I'd been missing until Sadie opened my eyes.

In our never-ending quest to find new and more effective treatments and therapies for Sadie, at the end of September we began what's called "muscle testing" with Marty Johnson at Total Health. Muscle testing is a type of holistic alternative treatment that is normally done on humans but can be performed on animals as well. When performed on humans, the patient can either stand up or lie down. Then he or she holds up an arm while the practitioner holds a vial containing a vitamin or mineral near the specific body system being tested while simultaneously pushing down on the person's arm. If the arm lacks strength and resistance and can be pushed down, then the person is lacking in the vitamin or mineral that's contained in the vial.

When muscle testing is performed on an animal, a human is used as a surrogate. The surrogate would place his or her hand on Sadie while the practitioner held the vial with the vitamin or mineral close to Sadie's various body parts, then pressed on the surrogate's arm to gauge the resistance. Depending on how the person's arm reacted, the practitioner could determine what elements Sadie was lacking.

I saw muscle testing as yet another way to keep Sadie in balance, making sure that she was getting the essential vitamins and nutrients that would balance and complement her special diet and her grueling therapy and exercises. When I had said at the beginning that I was "all-in" where Sadie was concerned, I meant that I was all-in on the very deepest level. There was nothing I would not do for her, no road I would not go down, no idea I would not explore. She was worth it, a fact she proved to me every day.

Sadie and I had had such an amazing experience at the PrideFest parade that summer that I began to think about taking Sadie to Mardi Gras in New Orleans to take part in the famous pet parade. I'd never gone any farther than Madison with Sadie, a ninety-minute drive from home, but I knew that we needed to expand her horizons if we were going to gain support and spread her message beyond just southeast Wisconsin. What Sadie had to teach people about overcoming obstacles and never giving up was too important to limit it to one relatively small geographic region.

So I began looking for flights from Milwaukee to New Orleans that accepted dogs and allowed them to travel in the cabin with the passengers rather than in a cage in the cargo hold. Sadie, because of her special needs, would never be able to cope with the trauma of being placed beneath the plane in the cargo hold, which is why I needed her at my side, so I could observe her during the flight.

I looked into mercy flights and angel flights but they didn't cover situations like Sadie's. The people I contacted were invariably kind, but they would tell me, "We help disabled people, not disabled dogs," or "We only rescue dogs from floods." So I turned my attention to the major U.S. commercial airlines. Based on my research, it looked like they all had a forty-pound limit for dogs allowed in the cabin; heavier dogs were required to travel in cargo, and Sadie was now well over that forty-pound limit.

Undaunted, I began contacting the airlines directly via email. My emails began with, "I'm interested in taking a flight to New Orleans with my dog, Sadie. Let me tell you a little bit about Sadie first. She was found in Kentucky after being shot in the head and the back after delivering a litter of puppies . . ." People needed to be introduced to Sadie, they needed to know her background and her story to understand why this was so important.

Every person I contacted replied personally and said, "What an amazing story." But even though they were touched and amazed by Sadie's story, they were unable to help. So I put this project on hold for the moment, but I had every intention of coming back to it in the not-too-distant future. Sadie was clearly ready to spread her wings, in more ways than one.

Later that autumn Dr. Jodie recommended that we take Sadie to be evaluated and assessed at the prestigious University of Wisconsin School of Veterinary Medicine in Madison. Dr. Jodie wasn't concerned that anything in particular might be wrong or that Sadie was failing to make progress in her rehab. She simply felt that now that we had been working with Sadie so intensely for eighteen months, this would be a great time to get a second opinion about where Sadie was, rehab-wise, if there were other treatments and therapies that we should be trying, and what her prospects and prognosis looked like for the future.

I thought this was a fantastic idea and couldn't wait to do it. I had always felt that there was a missing piece in terms of Sadie's ability to walk, something that, if we could just figure out what it was and address it, would allow her to ambulate again like a normal dog.

We were able to arrange an appointment for the end of October. I was really excited and optimistic, looking forward to what the doctors would say and to finally getting Sadie some much-deserved answers.

Looking back at it now, I realize I probably should have taken the weather that day as an omen for what was to come. It was Halloween, Thursday, October 31. The wind howled, dark clouds massed overhead, and intermittent sheets of rain lashed my SUV as Dr. Jodie, Sadie, and I drove the hour and a half to Madison. Sadie was her usual curious, chipper self as she sat up straight and tall in the back with her nose pressed to the window, her breath fogging the glass as she intently watched the world flying by.

The appointment itself lasted for several hours as Sadie was tested and evaluated by a team of neurologists and several other veterinary specialists. As this was a teaching hospital there were also dozens of veterinary students there observing and coming in and out of the exam rooms at all times, adding to the chaotic atmosphere.

Sometimes Dr. Jodie and I were allowed to be in the room with Sadie and sometimes not, depending on what they were doing to her, but Sadie was a trouper regardless, even when one of the vets pressed down as hard as possible on Sadie's back legs to gauge her pain response. As a mom, it was really hard for me to watch my baby being forced to endure this, even though intellectually I understood that it was a necessary part of the examination. I couldn't wait to take Sadie home and give her extra kisses and cuddles that night, along with all kinds of treats for being such a good girl.

The vets seemed especially interested in evaluating how Sadie walked, or tried to walk, as they placed her on the floor and she demonstrated, reaching forward with her front paws. Her back end moved up and in, propelled forward by her upper body as her lower body followed with her left leg dragging behind on the ground.

As the doctors watched and took notes, Sadie traversed the length of the exam room. They also asked a lot of detailed questions about Sadie's diet, therapy, treatments, and exercises. I emphasized how we had focused on maintaining her upper body strength to help compensate for what her lower body lacked. I also told them about her wagon and the Walkin' Wheels, which she still hadn't embraced, even though we worked with them a few hours every week, trying to increase her comfort with the device.

When at last all the testing and evaluation was finished, I asked Dr. Jodie how she thought it had gone. The doctors had promised to email me the full results in a few days, so I was just looking for her first impressions rather than anything definitive.

"I thought it went really well," she said with a satisfied nod. "I'm interested to hear what they thought, but I'm not expecting any major surprises."

"I hope you're right," I replied. "I'm just hoping they have some new ideas and recommendations for what it will take to get Sadie walking again."

Over the next few days I was so busy scheduling Sadie's meet-and-greets and arranging interviews and media coverage for her upcoming appearances and events that I almost forgot about our trip to Madison. I just happened to be checking my email late on Saturday afternoon, November 2, when I saw that I'd received something from the UW-Madison School of Veterinary Medicine. *Okay!* I thought excitedly. *At last we'll get some answers!*

After reading the brief cover letter, I downloaded and opened the attached pdf. Nothing in the world could have prepared me for what greeted me inside that document. The words stole my breath away, shattering my heart into a million little pieces. Some of the medical and veterinary jargon was hard to interpret, but most of what was written couldn't be clearer:

DIAGNOSIS

L4-S1 myelopathy
Paraplegic, deep pain negative
Secondary to historical gunshot and shrapnel injury

COMMENTS

Sadie has no deep pain or voluntary motor in either pelvic limbs. The motions she makes with the hind limbs when she tries to walk is a reflex called "spinal walking" that she is unable to voluntarily control. Unfortunately, the chronic nature of her injuries and neurologic status indicate that she will never be able to
regain the ability to feel her feet or walk voluntarily with her pelvic limbs.

I stopped reading. I stopped breathing. *Never be able to regain the ability to feel her feet or walk voluntarily*. No. No. No. My spirits were crushed. Not my Sadie. Please, God, how can this be? I've spent literally every waking moment of the past eighteen months working with Sadie to get her walking again. And now the doctors are saying that will never happen. They are telling us there is no hope. Has all this been for nothing, then?

Forcing my eyes back to the screen, I continued to, "Additional instructions and comments."

> Sadie's ability to move about unassisted is
> wonderful to see. Unfortunately, we have no thera-
> pies to offer that will bring back the
> ability to use her pelvic limbs voluntarily.
> E-stim or other therapies directed towards
> regaining voluntary motor of her pelvic limbs are
> unlikely to have any effect.

No therapies to offer . . . unlikely to have any effect. I reread those words as my eyes burned with tears. Steeling all the courage I could, I scrolled to the final page and read the results of the physical exam:

> Non-ambulatory paraplegic. Able to walk on tho-
> racic limbs while dragging pelvic limbs . . . Severe
> muscle atrophy of pelvic limb
> musculature.

Non-ambulatory paraplegic. The vets are calling my baby a paraplegic. A paraplegic who will never walk again. How dare they steal her hope?

Devastated, I logged off, closed the computer, and went downstairs, where Sadie was relaxing, snoozing beside

Sparky as they spooned in a patch of sunlight, so rare and so welcome on a November late afternoon. I sat down next to Sadie and pulled her into my lap. "I'm so sorry, Sadie," I whispered gently, stroking her head. "But I'm not ready to give up on you. Doctors are often wrong. Remember all the experts who said you'd be urinary and fecally incontinent forever? Well, you proved them wrong. The experts can be wrong about this, too."

As I stroked her head and massaged her shoulders, I felt the deep heat of her fur where the sun had done its magic, warming her deep down to the skin. She turned her head and gazed up at me with her soft, drowsy, golden amber eyes, blinking slowly.

Suddenly I recalled something Keri Davis had said during her reading of Sadie. Keri had emphasized that Sadie's journey was more about her changing me, forcing me to open my mind and my heart, than it was about me rehabbing her, or returning her to the state of physical wholeness that she'd existed in before she'd been shot. That was the message I'd been missing, the real message embedded deep within Keri's words. "Sustain Sadie, support her, and let her be who she needs to be," Keri had insisted. "Where there is acceptance, true healing begins."

"Oh Sadie, why did it take me so long to understand?" I asked in a broken voice. "You *are* whole; you are perfect just the way you are. You are perfect even if you never walk again. You have been perfect from the day I first found you."

I was the one who was lacking, not Sadie. I was the one so focused on one goal, getting her walking again, that I totally missed the big picture. But now the scales had fallen from my eyes and the truth appeared to me with crystal clarity. "We're no longer going to wait, wait until you're perfect, until you're healed, until you can walk again," I promised Sadie. "The next phase of your life starts right now. Your mission is too important to postpone any longer. You don't need to stand on four legs in order to get your message across."

I hugged her again, holding her close and pressing my chin against her forehead. "Thank you, my perfect Sadie, for being just the way you are. Thank you for being my greatest teacher, and for teaching me the most valuable lesson of all."

CHAPTER ELEVEN
Going Gaga for GooFurr

The results from our meeting with the neurologists in Madison were devastating, but in truth I hardly had time to think about that as we moved into the 2013 holiday season. This year the holidays were even busier than they had been during Sadie's first Christmas with me the year before. We sent out over five hundred Christmas cards to friends and supporters around the country and around the world as more and more people had joined our mailing lists and donated funds at the credit union or online.

We marched in several Christmas parades that season, including the Muskego Christmas parade, for which our friend Beth decorated Sadie's wagon so it looked like a sleigh while Sadie dressed up as Santa with a red stocking cap and fake white beard. I, of course, dressed as one of Santa's reindeer, pulling "Santa" in her sleigh!

Events like these weren't just fun ways to get out and meet people; they served an important marketing purpose as well. I had enlisted the help of numerous "elves" to hand out little packages of Dr. Jodie's natural pet treats along with Sadie information cards to people along the parade route, introducing more and more people to Sadie's remarkable story.

Sadie was also invited to participate in the Trees of Hope charity event that Christmas. We were given the opportunity to create a Christmas tree with a Saving Sadie theme, and then beautiful ornaments for that tree were made and donated by Sadie supporters all over the world. Once Sadie's and all the other trees were decorated, the trees were auctioned off, with the money raised going toward cancer research. Sadie's supporters were beyond generous in this cause and we received literally hundreds of stunning ornaments for her tree.

The Trees of Hope charity was founded by Karen and Gene Wenzel in honor of their daughter, Lindsay, who died of leukemia in 2010 at the age of thirty-two. It meant so much to Sadie and me to be a part of something like this; although what the Wenzel family endured was very different from Sadie's situation, we shared with them the desire to promote hope and healing, and to create something positive out of personal despair.

During this season we were also doing tons of meet-and-greets, especially at Pet World and other stores that were jam-packed with holiday shoppers, and we had started visiting a number of local businesses as well to do meet-and-greets with employees and staff. Sadie just has such a special ability to inspire people and cheer them up; a boring old office full of tired and overstressed employees was transformed into a party as soon as I entered wheeling Sadie in her wagon.

I couldn't believe how much fun Sadie and I were having. I had expected I'd be starting to wind down by this time in my life, cutting back, thinking about retirement. Instead, I was busier, more active, more engaged, and more fulfilled than ever. I was working on something so much bigger than me now, and that made waking up each day a new and exciting adventure. It was an honor and a privilege to be the one helping Sadie work her magic.

I never would have imagined, that day at the shelter back in 2012, that this was where we'd end up. I thought I was going to rehab a disabled dog; I never dreamed I'd be changing the world. But Sadie was a force to be reckoned with, and I was just grateful that she had chosen me to join her on the ride.

But even with all the fun we were having, the hard work of rehab never let up. Despite the discouraging prognosis from the vets at the University of Wisconsin hospital, we chose not only to continue Sadie's intense treatments, exercise, and therapies, but actually to increase our efforts. I still believed there was a chance that Sadie could regain enough strength and feeling in her spine and back legs to walk again, even though that was no longer our primary goal. Sadie had already proven the experts wrong so many times before.

And if it were true that she would never walk again—*especially* if she never walked again—it was vitally important that she maintain as much strength, flexibility, and mobility in her limbs and upper body as possible, so she could continue doing all the things she *could* do. Therefore, her schedule never slackened as she kept pace with swimming, acupuncture, aqua puncture, e-stim, physical therapy, massage, and our various at-home exercises.

We had also gotten some new, custom-made braces for Sadie's back legs from a place called Paws to Embrace. She made it clear she did not love them, but they were useful, especially in helping her to stand when we did exercises that involved stretching and reaching for spoonfuls of peanut butter.

Sadie was also still taking more than twenty-five vitamins, minerals, and supplements twice every day. It usually took me about forty-five minutes per session to get all these pills and tablets into her, by hiding them in raw meat and feeding her each pill individually with a special spoon. I never knew for sure how many of the pills actually ended up inside of Sadie and how many of them ended up on the kitchen floor.

But then Dr. Jodie introduced me to a new product she was carrying at the clinic called GooFurr and suggested Sadie and I try it. GooFurr was a delivery system for pills and supplements. It had been designed primarily for cats but worked just as well with dogs. GooFurr comes in a tube and is a paste made of smoked wild salmon, cornstarch, and water. The pill or supplement is crushed into powder, mixed with the GooFurr paste, and then fed to the animal (or, in the case of cats, the paste mixture can also be spread onto the fur where the cat will lick it off and thereby ingest the vitamin or supplement).

When I took GooFurr home and tried it, Sadie loved it immediately! Perhaps because she loved canned cat food so much, the salmon flavor of the paste appealed to her right away and she happily consumed her crushed-up pills. For me the product was a godsend, cutting down my dosing time with Sadie from forty-five to ten minutes per session, freeing up more than an hour of my day in total time saved.

I was so impressed with the product that I wrote to the inventor and founder of GooFurr, Barbara Capelli, and asked her if I might get a discount on GooFurr if I ordered in bulk. She very kindly sent me a large shipment of the product, and we started a casual correspondence. Just a few weeks later she asked me out of the blue, "How would Sadie like to become the official celebrity 'spokes-puppy' for GooFurr? That way you could join me in Hollywood in January to help promote GooFurr at the gifting party before the Golden Globe awards."

What? The Golden Globes? I was floored. I hadn't known Barbara long, but I was intrigued by the possibility. Barbara explained that GooFurr had been selected to be one of the products given away in the "swag bags" at the gifting party that would be held for celebrities and other VIPs at a swanky Beverly Hills hotel the day before the Golden Globes awards ceremony. I wouldn't be able to bring Sadie along, unfortunately, but I could bring Sadie's business cards, flyers, and postcards, and talk to as many people as possible, not just about how much Sadie loved GooFurr, but also about Sadie's story overall, further raising her profile at the national level.

This was just too good an opportunity to miss and we quickly made arrangements for the trip. Barbara, who's originally from Italy, was now living in Hawaii so we met in Los Angeles. It took some juggling to rearrange my work schedule and also make arrangements for Jeff to babysit Sadie, Sparky, Miss Kitty, and Kit Kat while I was away, but, happily, all the pieces fell into place.

When Barbara and I finally met in person at our hotel in

Los Angeles, we clicked immediately, and I knew Team Sadie
had just discovered another very valuable member. Barbara
was an unassuming, earthy woman with thick, brown,
shoulder-length hair and a lovely, mellifluous Italian accent.
The gifting party itself was incredible, held on January 11,
the day before the Golden Globes award ceremony, upstairs
at the Andaz West Hollywood hotel on Sunset Boulevard. I
saw more celebrities than I could name, and had a chance to
talk to Jo Anne Worley of the '60s TV show *Laugh-In* and
Joan Van Ark from *Knots Landing*.

The gifting party was truly a whirlwind experience,
something like a very upscale trade show, as we set up our
display in a large ballroom with plush carpeting and low, elegant light, and spent the whole day talking to hundreds of
party guests—actors and actresses and behind-the-scenes
Hollywood people—and handing out gift bags, promoting
GooFurr to everyone we met. Everyone who received a gift
bag received a complimentary tube of GooFurr, along with
a postcard insert with Sadie's photo, her testimonial about
the product, and our Saving Sadie website URL.

If I'd thought I'd connected with a lot of new people and
widened Sadie's sphere of influence at our local Christmas
parades and other events, I could only imagine how much
farther our message was being broadcast now. Sometimes I
had to pinch myself. Here I was, just an unassuming girl
from small town Wisconsin, rubbing shoulders with Hollywood's movers-and-shakers and the entertainment industry
elite.

And it's all because of Sadie, I thought, then sent up a
silent prayer for the angels to watch over her and keep her

safe while I was gone. The truth was, I really missed her and my three other fur babies, and couldn't wait to get back home to see them again and tell them all about my trip.

Barbara and I barely had a free moment to talk during the party, but when we had dinner at our hotel later that night, she asked me if I'd like to join her for another gifting party, this time at the pre-Oscars party in Hollywood in March. I immediately said yes, even without being sure I could juggle my work schedule and arrange pet-sitting with Jeff. *I'll find a way to make it work somehow*, I promised myself. *Opportunities like this don't come around every day, and I've learned from Sadie that sometimes you just need to take that leap of faith, cross your fingers (and paws!), and have confidence that it will all work out.*

On my flight to California for the Oscars gifting party a few weeks later, I sat next to a beautiful, vivacious young woman named Lisa who was traveling with her boyfriend, and also with her dog, a scruffy little mutt named Angel. We got to talking and I was intrigued to find out how she'd gotten permission to bring her dog on board the flight. She explained that Angel was traveling as a "comfort animal" that she needed to have with her so she felt able to fly.

I didn't want to pry by asking her what specific condition she needed the dog for, but the seed was definitely planted in my mind in terms of how I might be able to fly with Sadie and get permission for her to sit with me in the cabin. *Hmmm, comfort animal*, I thought. *Sadie certainly fits* that *bill.*

Our experience at the pre-Oscars gifting party on the first of March was very similar to our experience at the party before the Golden Globes—a whirlwind of meeting people, spotting celebrities (*Could that be Tom Cruise standing in the corner?*), talking about Sadie, promoting GooFurr, and handing out free samples. The party was held at the Montage Beverly Hills, a luxury five-star hotel just off the famed Rodeo Drive, and again as we set up inside the elegant ballroom, I was in absolute awe of the glamour, money, prestige, and influence parading before our eyes.

One of the people who stopped by to chat with us was Carolyn Hennesy, the Emmy-Award-nominated actress from *General Hospital* and *True Blood*. Carolyn is also a deeply committed animal rights activist who hosts her own syndicated radio show, *Animal Magnetism*. We got to talking and Carolyn fell in love with Sadie's story. She couldn't wait to book Sadie and me as call-in guests on her show, and we promised to make arrangements as soon as we were both back home and could compare calendars. As Carolyn walked away and I looked down at her business card in my hand, I thought about what an extraordinary adventure I was on; the only thing that could have made it better would have been having Sadie there with me, along to enjoy this wild, crazy, exciting ride.

At the end of this second brief trip to California, Barbara had yet another surprise for me up her sleeve. She had been invited to appear on the morning talk show *The Balancing Act* on cable TV's Lifetime network to talk about GooFurr, and she wanted me to come along. Only this time, she asked me to bring Sadie, too, so Sadie could be part of an in-studio demonstration showing viewers how to use GooFurr.

Rather than another trip to California, this would instead involve a trip to Pompano Beach, Florida, where *The Bal-*

ancing Act was filmed. If I said yes, we'd need to make arrangements quickly because they planned to film the segment on March 18 and it was already March 2.

Yes, I told Barbara as we shared a taxi to the airport, *let's do it. I'm not sure about the logistics, but I'm willing to take that leap of faith to make it happen.* Sadie had already made numerous local TV appearances, but national television exposure had always been one of our "bucket list" goals. Now, at last, it was about to happen. *The magic of Sadie*, I thought as I sat back in my seat and smiled. *There she goes again, making amazing things happen.*

As soon as I got home, my first task was to figure out how to make Sadie my "companion animal" on the flight to Florida. I did some research online and learned that companion animals are technically known as Emotional Support Animals (ESA) and that any animal, dog, cat, bird, hamster, and so forth, could fill the role. ESAs did not need to be service animals or have any special training, they only had to be well behaved and "provide therapeutic benefit to its owner through companionship and affection." Well that described Sadie to a T!

In order for an animal to travel as an ESA, the owner had to have a letter from a doctor or registered therapist stating the person's diagnosis and recommending the use of an ESA. Fortunately, this process could all be done online. I paid my fee, downloaded the questionnaire, filled it out, and emailed it back to be reviewed by a therapist. Following the review of the questionnaire came a phone interview with a registered therapist, who asked me a lot of questions about why I felt I couldn't travel without Sadie.

I thought I did a pretty good job with my answers, explaining why I needed Sadie close to me to comfort and support me while I flew, but obviously, I was wrong—at the end of the phone interview, the therapist informed me that, in her estimation, I did not "suffer from an ailment that would benefit from the presence of an Emotional Support Animal." *Ouch*. Well, at least they refunded my application fee.

If I had learned one thing from Sadie (and in truth I had learned thousands of things from Sadie), it was to never give up, to keep trying, no matter what, so, undaunted, I applied for the ESA certificate again, paid the fee once more, downloaded and completed the questionnaire, and waited for another phone interview with a therapist (happily, it was a different therapist this time).

In this second interview I tried to sound more emotional and melodramatic, emphasizing that I couldn't leave Sadie alone because I feared that someone would hurt her, that we had never been separated because I relied on her to help me manage my stress, et cetera. I really laid it on thick, and it must have worked, because this time, I passed the test! Apparently, in the span of a few days, I had managed to develop an ailment serious enough to require help! Yay, me!

Three days later, I received an email with the pdf letter from the therapist certifying that Sadie was my Emotional Support Animal and that I needed her with me when I traveled.

Letter in hand, I phoned Southwest Airlines and arranged a flight for Sadie and me to Fort Lauderdale for mid-March. When I explained that I'd be traveling with my companion animal, this time they said, "Okay, no problem. A representative from the airline will meet you at the airport." It really was that simple.

"All right, Sadie, you've got southeastern Wisconsin in your back pocket," I told her as I sat beside her on the floor and stroked her firmly from head to tail. "Now it's time for the rest of the country to fall in love with you, too." Of course, actually getting her on the plane and all the way to a TV studio in Florida twelve hundred miles away would bring lots more challenges, I realized, but we were ready for it. Sadie was proving every day that there was nothing she couldn't do once she set her mind to it.

CHAPTER TWELVE
Florida, Here We Come

At last the day dawned, Sunday, March 16, for the trip to Florida to film our segment for *The Balancing Act* on cable TV's Lifetime channel. I was so excited for Sadie to spread her wings (no pun intended) and experience this new adventure. We were up early, packed, organized, and on our way to Milwaukee's Mitchell Field for our direct flight to Fort Lauderdale after saying good-bye to Jeff, who had kindly agreed to babysit for Sparky, Miss Kitty, and Kit Kat over the next couple of days.

Amidst all the whirlwind of activity, I had taken time to bathe Sadie the night before, so she would be even-more-than-her-usual beautiful when she made her national TV debut. I really wanted her to shine when the camera was on her, glowing bright and healthy beneath the lights for all the world to see.

It had been nearly two years since she'd had the surgery to remove the bullet from her forehead and the cyst from her tail, so it had been a long time since I'd placed her in my bathtub and washed her like a child, but I did again this night, filling the tub half full with warm water and some lavender essential oil, then lifting Sadie in my arms and carefully lowering her in until her limbs and lower body were covered. She seemed surprised that we were doing this again, as she gazed straight at me with her soft, round, amber eyes, large and dilated in the low evening light. And yet within those eyes I recognized patience, trust, and above all else, love. "It's okay, girl," I reassured her. "Every celebrity diva should get a little pampering before her big day."

I rubbed some baby shampoo between my palms and gently soaped her up, squeezing the suds through her thick, wet fur and rinsing with cups of water. For the first time since Barbara suggested the trip to Florida, I began to have some doubts. Sadie was always so mellow; nothing ever seemed to faze her, but we had never tried something like this before. *What if it's too much for her? What if she becomes traumatized and starts to panic? What if we just can't get her on the plane?* I wondered, had this been a crazy, stupid idea right from the beginning?

I took Sadie's left front paw in my hand and gently washed it with a soft cloth, then washed the left, cleaning carefully between her toes. *It's not too late to cancel,* I thought suddenly. *Barbara would be disappointed, but she could do the show without me. If I phoned her tonight, she'd have time to find someone else. I'm sure she would understand.*

As I started on Sadie's back paws, she nudged me with her snout to get my attention. It was almost like she was saying, "Don't give up on me, Mom. Don't give up on us." I had promised Sadie I would never quit, would never let her down. How could I go back on that now? "If we don't go to Florida," it was like Sadie was saying, "we risk missing out on something amazing."

"You're right, Boo-boo," I said as I rinsed the last of the

shampoo and began to drain the tub. "If we back out now, we might miss something amazing. You've taught me to never be afraid of saying yes. You've taught me to embrace every opportunity with open arms."

The next morning, I made sure I had my Emotional Support Animal certificate in my purse; in fact, I had printed three copies and stashed them in various places on my person and around my luggage, just to be safe. I had never done anything like this trip before, and we couldn't afford any last-minute glitches.

When we got to the airport, the representative from Southwest, a fortysomething woman in a crisp orange, red, and blue uniform with her hair pulled back tightly in a bun, met us at a restaurant inside the airport as promised and we went over the logistics of actually getting Sadie onto the plane. Sadie utterly charmed the rep, sitting up in her wagon, squaring her shoulders, wagging her tail, eyes blazing as she seemed to follow our conversation.

"Oh, who's a good girl; are you a good girl?" the woman cooed, pursing her lips and squishing Sadie's face between her palms, bringing her nose close to Sadie's snout. "Who's a very good girl?"

Sadie barked and I stifled a laugh. Sadie was a natural mood-elevator, reducing middle-aged professionals to quivering bowls of puppy-loving Jell-O. After Sadie and the rep said their au revoirs, we made our way to the ticket counter, checked in for the flight, and passed through security, all without a hitch, even getting Sadie and her wagon through the metal detector. *If it's always this easy,* I thought, *we could travel a lot more, and a lot farther. Just think about all the new doors that might open for Sadie.*

We waited in the departure lounge for our flight to be called. The other passengers milling about were very curious about the black-and-tan dog in the special Saving Sadie wagon, and soon we had a throng of people stopping by to chat. I handed out Sadie's business card to everyone within reach as I shared Sadie's story.

Some people expressed surprise that I was actually taking a disabled dog on a commercial air flight, so I used this opportunity to emphasize Sadie's message about focusing on what you *can* do, not what you can't. As the people walked away, I imagined them carrying Sadie's message with them, like seeds of hope stuck to their skin, ready to be disbursed and take root in destinations across the country and around the world. This was the best sort of ripple effect—one touch from Sadie ultimately affecting people miles and miles away.

A woman's voice over the loudspeaker announced that our flight had begun pre-boarding anyone traveling with young children, the elderly, or others with special needs who required a little extra time. "That's us, Boo-boo," I told Sadie as I grabbed our bags and the handle of her wagon and pulled us through the departure gate and into the breezeway that connected the gate to the airplane.

I couldn't maneuver Sadie's wagon through the doorway, into the plane, and down the aisle, so I parked Sadie in her wagon in the breezeway near the door. Beth, who had made the insert for Sadie's Christmas sled, had also sewn a fantastic travel mat for Sadie, a tri-folding collapsible rectangle of fabric that worked as a liner in her wagon and could then be unfolded and refolded to make a mat for Sadie to sit on on the floor of the cabin at my feet during the flight.

So, leaving behind Sadie in her wagon, I grabbed the mat, went in and found us a seat in the bulkhead (Southwest doesn't do assigned seats, so I got to choose where we sat), stowed our luggage, and unfolded and put down the mat on the floor in front of my seat. Then I went back, got Sadie, carried her into the plane, settled her on the mat, went back out again, folded up the wagon, and checked it with the cabin crew.

Whew! I was exhausted, and we hadn't even left yet. "Next time," I told Sadie, catching my breath as I buckled my seat belt, "we'll fly first class, and your entourage can handle the logistics of getting you on board. We'll leave it up to your 'people.'" After all, if Sadie was going to be a celebrity, she would have "people," right?

Sadie had remained her normal relaxed, happy, chipper self throughout all the noise and stress and commotion of the morning, never bothered by all the new and confusing sights, sounds, and smells. It was only as the engines started to roar beneath our feet when we prepared to take off that she began showing some nerves.

I think the vibrations from the engines actually bothered her more than the noise. Fortunately, I had brought along some essential oil, Peace & Calming, just in case, so I poured a little into the palm of my hand, warmed it up, and gently massaged her, which really helped to soothe her and settle her nerves.

Airline rules only required that Sadie remain on the floor during takeoff and landing, so once we reached cruising altitude I lifted her from the floor and sat her in the window seat beside me. We had the full three-seat row in the bulkhead to ourselves, so we were able to move around without annoying other passengers.

Once Sadie was in her seat she pressed her nose to the window and watched everything with intense interest, just as she would do in my SUV. I so wished she could tell me what she was seeing, how the world looked to her, before the plane pierced the heavy cloud cover and the stormy, dark blue-gray surface of southern Lake Michigan disappeared from view.

It was incredible to think that Sadie had been destined to live out her life locked in a cold metal cage in a lonely animal shelter, her only view that of bare concrete floors and walls, and the shadowy figures of other animals that had also been abandoned and unloved. And now, here she was, soaring through the sky, quickly gaining altitude and stretching toward thirty-five thousand feet above the earth.

The flight to Fort Lauderdale lasted just under three hours. When we landed, I waited for the plane to empty, then I left Sadie on the floor, took her mat, and went to get her wagon, which was waiting, tagged and folded, in the breezeway just beyond the door. I unfolded and set up the wagon, arranged the fabric insert, and parked it near the door. Then I went back, got Sadie, and carried her to the wagon. As I wheeled her and our luggage down the breezeway to the gate, I felt a sense of both amazement and relief. We did it! Sadie had flown twelve hundred miles, nearly the full length of the country from north to south, from the cold, hard freeze of late spring Wisconsin to the lush, fragrant, citrus-scented tropics of the Florida coast. "For a dog that's supposedly disabled, Boo-boo," I told her, "you sure do get around!"

Barbara, who had earlier flown in from Hawaii, was waiting to pick us up in front of the airport. When she and Sadie met, it was love at first sight! Barbara had invited Sadie to be GooFurr's "spokes-puppy" without ever meeting her in person, so it was especially gratifying to see how well they hit it off! If Sadie could talk, I knew she would thank Barbara for inventing something that made it so much easier to take her pills and supplements, and she would especially thank her for making it in her favorite flavor—cat food salmon!

We had booked our rooms at a pet-friendly hotel, but once we arrived I realized that "pet-friendly" did not necessarily mean "Sadie-friendly." Once we checked in at the front desk, we had to wheel Sadie in her wagon through the whole hotel, then struggle to get the wagon across the sand to the other building where our room was located, then up the elevator and down a long hallway to our room. When Sadie needed a potty break, I had to pack her up in the wagon, go down the hall, down the elevator, outside, and through the sand to a private place where she could relieve herself. Definitely a huge hassle.

That night Barbara, Sadie, and I went to dinner at a restaurant (pet-friendly, or so they said) on the water and had a lovely meal, soaking up the warm, fresh, Atlantic breezes and listening to the sizzle of the surf slapping the sand. "Thank you," I said to Barbara as I sliced into my grilled red snapper. "This is a dream come true."

"To Sadie," she said in her melodious Italian accent, raising her glass of wine in a toast. "Tomorrow, she will make us proud."

The next morning we were up early and Barbara drove

us the forty-five minutes to the O2 Media studio complex in Pompano Beach, where *The Balancing Act* and several other Lifetime shows are filmed. My nerves were a little jangly as we entered the building, wheeling Sadie in her wagon, but everyone on the staff was fantastic and quickly put us all at ease. We were taken to the green room and briefed by one of the show's production staff. The host of *The Balancing Act*, Olga Villaverde, a slim, glamorous woman with dark eyes and long black hair, popped her head in to introduce herself and say hi, which also helped calm our nerves.

While Barbara was in hair and makeup, I got Sadie ready for the show, draping her in her big fluffy green-and-yellow feather boa and securing around her neck her special "bling" collar, black fabric studded with rows of glittering rhinestones. The yellow-and-green color scheme was intentional; her wagon was draped in her signature yellow-and-green fabric cover with SAVINGSADIE.COM on the sides, along with the most well-known photo of her, the close-up of her face from when the bullet hole in her forehead was still visible. I wore a white cowl-neck sweater and yellow blazer to complement the overall color scheme.

Then it was time to go on set to start the taping. "Okay, Sadie," I told her, bending down to whisper in her ear, "it's show time."

The set itself was deceptively small, designed to look like a casual, contemporary living room with a hardwood floor, faux-brick wall, tall potted plants, and a false window, lit from behind, displaying *The Balancing Act* title and logo. The director positioned Barbara and me side by side on the beige sofa with large, overstuffed pillows propping up our backs, while Olga sat in a chair beside our sofa. Sadie stayed in her wagon, parked directly in front of us.

The red light glowed above camera number one as the director cued Olga and called out, "Action." With a deep breath and a dazzling smile, Olga looked straight into the camera and began. "This morning I would like to share with you an *amazing* story about an *amazing* dog, who was shot twice, left for dead, but was given a second chance and beat the odds. Let's take a look."

The camera moved in close on Sadie in her wagon and I watched as she gazed straight into the camera, the green and yellow feathers of her boa fluttering around her face. Olga continued in a somber voiceover as the camera lingered on Sadie, *After having her litter of puppies, she was found in the mountains, barely alive. Someone shot her between the eyes and in her back. Sadie was left there to die.*

A photo montage of Sadie's key moments played out on the screen, a photo showing her with the stitches in her head after her surgery, scenes of her swimming, trying out her leg braces, and exercising on the trampoline. *Sadie was taken to the hospital, her prognosis grim; her chances of survival, not good,* Olga explained over the pictures.

After Olga summarized the rest of Sadie's story, the scene returned to the studio and Olga introduced Barbara and me. "Joal, let me start with you." Olga pivoted toward me. "How is Sadie doing now?"

"It's been an incredible journey, Olga," I replied. "It's just been amazing. From the day I picked her up, she's just taught me so very much. Sadie just absolutely absorbs life, and she teaches other people, too, about acceptance."

"You know what's amazing, and we've talked about this on the phone before you came here; you told me that emotionally she's been through so much, and yet she's a happy dog," Olga marveled.

"She's amazingly happy," I emphasized. "She has no memory whatsoever of what happened to her."

Then Olga asked me about Sadie's medications and I showed her the shoebox I had brought from home that had bottles of all Sadie's pills and supplements. Olga looked astonished when I told her that Sadie took twenty-five pills twice every day, which gave us a nice segue into talking about GooFurr and the difference it had made in our lives.

Barbara then explained what GooFurr is and demonstrated how it works by taking one of Sadie's pills and crushing it with the back of a spoon until it was all powder, then squeezed out a length of GooFurr from the tube and mixed it well with a tiny spatula. "It camouflages the taste of the pill," Barbara explained, "you know, some pills taste worse than others."

Once the powder had been fully mixed into the paste, Barbara handed me the spatula with the GooFurr, I held it out to Sadie, and she licked it clean with three quick, committed swipes of her tongue. *Yes! Go Sadie! That's my girl—perfectly on cue, just like an old pro!* Having hit her mark, Sadie went back to relaxing in front of the camera, her chin resting contentedly on the edge of the wagon.

"For you, I can only imagine this was a lifesaver, Joal," Olga said.

"An absolute lifesaver," I replied. "Because you can only imagine, if Sadie takes this many pills per day, anybody out there, any viewer that has to give their dog or cat one or two pills a day, it's going to be an absolute godsend to them."

Our segment lasted a little over six minutes, but the whole interview seemed to pass in the blink of an eye as suddenly the director was signaling Olga to wrap it up. "Thank you. God bless you for saving her," Olga said to me, leaning closer and pressing her palms together as if in prayer. "When Sadie gets better, you come back and tell us how she's doing."

Her offer touched me deeply. "We will," I promised. "Thank you so much."

Barbara, Sadie, and I were all on cloud nine as we drove back to the hotel, giggling like schoolgirls about our exciting adventure. Since the show was taped and not live, they couldn't tell us for certain when it would actually be broadcast, but it would likely be at least another month or so. I couldn't wait for all of Sadie's fans around the country to have the chance to witness her in action, lighting up the screen.

Our time in Florida was brief as later that day we headed home. Getting back to Wisconsin proved to be a bit more difficult than getting to Florida had been. Once we arrived at the airport and checked our luggage, Sadie needed a potty break before the flight, but there was nowhere close by for her to go, so I wheeled her back outside toward the parking structure and found a motorcycle cop directing traffic. "This is my dog Sadie, and she really needs to go potty," I explained, "but she can't walk, so we need some help."

The cop very kindly stopped traffic in both directions and waved us across the road, where there was a small grassy knoll between sections of the parking structure—an ideal spot for Sadie to relieve herself. The cop was even kind enough to stop traffic for us on the way back to the terminal.

Once we were back inside the airport things were chaotic as no one from the airline had gotten the message that I was traveling with an Emotional Support Animal even though everything had supposedly been arranged before-hand. Fortunately, I had my ESA certificate in my purse, and as soon as I produced it, everything fell into place. Sadie, as usual, was a trouper, even as the TSA agents passed her wagon through the metal detector several times and then seemed to subject her to excessive wanding. What they thought she might be hiding, I cannot imagine.

The only disappointment I felt about our trip to Florida was the fact that I couldn't take Sadie to the beach. I had so hoped we could spend some time at the beach and she could dip her paws into the ocean, but the beach at Fort Lauderdale was so wide, and the sand so hot, soft, and deep, it was impossible to pull the wagon any distance. The wheels kept sinking into the pale yellow sand, and the shoreline was too far for me to carry Sadie there.

Despite what the vets in Madison had said, I still dreamed of someday watching Sadie run, wild and free, across a wide-open beach, sand flying from her feet, if not the ocean then closer to home, Milwaukee's Bradford Beach on Lake Michigan, with me throwing her a big stick or a Frisbee and she scrambling to grab it and bring it back to me clenched between her teeth.

"Maybe someday, Sadie," I told her as I buckled myself in for the return flight home. "I still believe that can happen. And even if it doesn't, you are free in so many other ways. Your spirit, your soul, they know no restriction."

CHAPTER THIRTEEN

Sadie Rides the *Seadog*

I don't believe in coincidences; I believe in kismet. I believe that things happen for a reason, that an invisible force, an unseen hand, is always working behind the scenes, guiding our lives, our paths, our destinies, from a place far beyond our limited comprehension. If not, then how else to explain the remarkable fact that our episode of *The Balancing Act* aired on Thursday, April 24, 2014, Sadie's second re-birthday, the two-year anniversary of the day our paths first crossed at the no-kill shelter in Kenosha?

We had filmed the segment in mid-March, so it could have aired any time after that. And yet, it aired on the morning of Sadie's special day. I had to believe it was fate that caused those special Sadie stars to align, fate that placed the planets in that unique and proper order.

I gathered all the animals into my bed early that cold spring morning and snuggled them close as the TV warmed up and *The Balancing Act*'s theme music kicked in at six thirty a.m. Normally I'd be up much earlier and already on my way to work at that hour, but I had taken the day off to help Sadie celebrate.

Seeing and hearing oneself on TV is always a strange experience, giving us rare insight into how we must look and sound to others. Our six-minute segment seemed to fly by just as quickly on television as it had live in the studio, but I was thrilled with how beautiful and expressive Sadie looked and how excellently she played to the camera. (I thought Barbara and I did pretty well, too—no obvious signs of the nerves we were both feeling!)

At the end of the segment our website URL was displayed prominently on the screen and Olga gave SavingSadie.com a nice mention as well. I was thrilled to think how many new people were now going to be coming to the website to find out more about Sadie.

Sure enough, the program had barely ended when my cell phone starting buzzing with congratulatory calls and texts from friends and contacts who had seen the show, and when I turned on my computer and logged in I saw we had been inundated with website hits and emails from people wanting to know more about Sadie. We also learned from staff at *The Balancing Act* that our segment was scheduled to run again on May 1, so even more people would see Sadie on screen and hear her important message.

We celebrated Sadie's second re-birthday privately that day, at home with just the five of us—me, Sadie, Sparky, Miss Kitty, and Kit Kat. I was planning to throw a huge public re-birthday party for her, even bigger than the one we'd had the year before, only this time in August, at an outdoor venue where other animals could attend to help celebrate with Sadie, and we could have food and live music, and raise lots of money for Sadie and for other good causes.

But that was down the road. For now, it was enough to spend quiet time alone with my fur babies, watching Sadie's star performance light up the TV. Sadie lay beside me, curled up in the blankets atop my bed, her eyes closed and face relaxed as I gently stroked her from head to tail.

Sadie, when I think back to that day two years ago, I barely recognize you as the dog I came across then. That dog was so thin, so filthy and terrified; that dead-eyed dog was just listless and vacant. To see you now, so big and bold and beautiful, so confident and outgoing, it's nothing short of miraculous. But I realized, with a start, that I no longer recognized the person I was two years ago, either. That person who thought she had it all but in fact had no idea what she was truly missing until Sadie came along.

On April 17 the *Wisconsin Gazette*, one of the state's largest LGBT publications, ran another long feature story about Sadie, beneath the headline, SHOT AND LEFT FOR DEAD, SADIE IS NOW A CHAMPION FOR ANIMAL WELFARE. The article summarized Sadie's background for readers who were unfamiliar with her story, and also gave an update on where she was now while describing our desire to work toward changes in the laws governing animal abuse and the punishment for perpetrators. I was touched to think how we had received such a warm welcome and support from the gay and lesbian community, who really connected with Sadie and took her to their hearts.

The *Wisconsin Gazette* article also yielded another unexpected benefit: it brought an incredible new member to Team Sadie, Kim Becker. Kim saw the article in the *Gazette* and immediately contacted me to offer us her services in helping Sadie's rehab. Kim's credentials were, frankly, mind-boggling.

A professional fitness, sports, and wellness specialist, Kim was one of the first women in the United States to be certified as an athletic trainer in the late 1970s. She had over thirty years of experience in the field and had worked with superstars such as Martina Navratilova, Steffi Graf, and the Chicago White Sox baseball team, and had even been invited to be part of the medical team for the 1984 Summer Olympics in Los Angeles.

Kim had never worked with animals before, she was strictly a trainer for humans, but she had been so moved by Sadie's story in the *Gazette* that she wanted to work with Sadie! What an incredible opportunity, not to mention yet another example of someone coming into my life and transforming it, and all because of Sadie.

Kim came to the house a few days after calling me about the article and she immediately put together a plan to work with Sadie two to three times a week, whenever she had time and could fit it in, either here at home or when I was at work and Sadie was at Jeff's. Her goal was to help Sadie improve her functioning both physically and mentally.

As you might expect of someone with her background, Kim was a tough taskmaster, but she was also a genius when it came to kicking up Sadie's exercises, adding push-ups and stretching, figuring out better ways to position her on the Power Plate, and thinking about how better to address the nerve and muscle damage in Sadie's back and legs. Kim was always looking for new things that we hadn't tried before. She firmly believed that stimulating Sadie's mind was as important as stimulating her body, so she devised many so-called Brain Games and activities to get Sadie thinking about and perceiving the world around her in new ways.

For example, Kim invented a shell game in which Sadie had to turn a wheel to figure out where a dog treat was hidden, and another game in which Sadie had to guess in which hand Kim held a treat. Kim also felt it was important for Sadie's brain development and sensory perception to experience fast movement, that sensation of hurtling forward, to remind her of what it felt like to run.

Kim would drag Sadie in her sled up to the top of a hill and then let her slide down, picking up speed until she was virtually airborne, ears back, tongue lolling, the wind in her face. Sadie loved these games and experiences, and I was touched to see the close bond she was developing with Kim, who was tough with Sadie when she needed to be, but who also understood the value in sometimes being tender.

By the summer of 2014, Sadie had been doing meet-and-greets and personal appearances for almost two years, speaking and presenting at stores, businesses, festivals, and so forth, in an informal way. We had also spoken at libraries and before various school groups, emphasizing Sadie's core message about accepting those beings, human and non-human, with disabilities and other special needs.

Even though we had been doing this work for a while, I wished to do a lot more, reaching more people with a more comprehensive and organized program and plan. Sadie had survived, she had been saved for a reason; she had an important message to send, while my own mission was to do everything I could to help her make that happen. We had waited long enough; it was time to get serious about this. I re-arranged my work schedule so I could do more client work at nights and on weekends, freeing up more time during the workweek, especially so we might become more involved with talking to kids at local schools.

Sadie and I put together a fifty-minute program that was appropriate for children of grade-school age and that could be presented in a school library or ordinary classroom. Our catchphrase became, "Think about what you can do, and not what you can't do, just like Sadie!"

I wanted kids to be able to get up close and personal with Sadie, to touch her, pet her, talk to her, to be able to see for themselves how she was different from other dogs, but also see that she was friendly and gentle and happy, just like any other dog. I wanted to show them that they shouldn't fear Sadie because she was different, just like they shouldn't fear adults or other kids who were different, either. I wanted to emphasize to the kids the importance of being kind to every living creature, human or animal.

Because this type of work was new to me, I had no idea where to begin in terms of contacting schools to see if they'd be interested in having Sadie and me come give our presentation. But Sadie had taught me that if you don't know how to do something, just jump right in anyway, because even if you fail you will have learned something just by trying. So I put together my project materials, a pitch letter email and pdf flyer, along with a laminated information sheet to hand out in person that described my presentation. I also created some Sadie-themed bookmarks, postcards, flyers, and business cards. Then I made a list of all the elementary schools in the Milwaukee and Waukesha districts and began a blanket campaign of contacting those schools via email.

As I expected, most of the schools didn't respond, or if they did, it was with a polite decline, but eventually I got my first nibble, when Garden Homes Lutheran School, a private elementary school in Milwaukee's inner city, invited us to come speak. The school was in one of the city's most socio-economically challenged neighborhoods, and yet all the students were well-behaved, energetic, and curious, looking absolutely adorable in their matching school uniforms of white shirts and black pants for the boys and white blouses and black jumpers for the girls.

The children's eyes all lit up when the teacher introduced us and I wheeled Sadie into the classroom. I could feel their energy bubbling over, so I made a point of saying, "Now, if you're really good, you'll get to pet Sadie at the end."

That was enough to convince them and they listened attentively as I talked about how Sadie was different from other dogs because she couldn't walk, but that she should be accepted, just like people who were different should be accepted. I was careful to be sensitive in how I presented Sadie's story to such a young and vulnerable audience. I made a point of saying that "bad people hurt Sadie," and that was why she couldn't walk, rather than say that she'd been shot. The sad reality was that many of these children had probably experienced or lost loved ones to gun violence in their lives, and they didn't need another reminder.

At the end of our presentation the kids got to pet Sadie as promised, and they descended on her wagon en masse, clamoring to get close to her, but Sadie, true to her nature, took it all in stride and patiently endured their very enthusiastic love and affection, sitting still and smiling for hugs and pets and kisses. Afterward the teacher took me aside and thanked me for the presentation, remarking on how great Sadie was with the kids and also how Sadie and I had found a unique way to spread a message that they themselves often struggled to get across.

Buoyed by the reaction to this organized school visit, I continued my marketing efforts in earnest and began booking more and more schools, along with libraries, community centers, and even some retirement homes and senior centers. While I used the same basic format for all my presentations, I also geared some of the details to the particular group we were meeting. I usually asked in advance if there was a specific message they wanted conveyed, whether it was about kindness or acceptance or something else.

Experience became my best teacher and I learned so much just by doing. For example, at one school our audience was a group of two- and three-year-olds. I told them how Sadie could now go potty on her own. As soon as I said that, a handful of little voices piped up, "I go potty." "I go potty now." "I go potty, too." Soon a chorus of enthusiastic potty-goers was happily sharing their status with the entire class. *Note to self—never mention "potty" to a group of toddlers.* It took some time to re-focus the audience's attention, primarily because the teachers were laughing so hard they could barely contain themselves.

I handled all the outreach, follow-up, scheduling, and planning for these events myself, and it was truly exhausting to add these tasks to my still-full-time day job and the hours of daily exercise and rehab I did with Sadie. Still, it felt incredibly rewarding, knowing we were fulfilling Sadie's mission, and I was always so humbled and touched when we got to a school and saw that the kids had made banners and signs to welcome Sadie, or when they gave us handmade thank-you notes before we went home.

That summer was full of fun and exciting events for Sadie and me, in addition to our meet-and-greets and presentations. In the middle of June we marched in our second Pride Parade at Milwaukee PrideFest, officially making it a yearly tradition (still continuing to this day). This year we had so many people from the LGBT community volunteer to join us in the march, distributing flyers and Sadie's business card, and as happened after the first year, we saw our biggest uptick in donations, web hits, retweets, Facebook likes, and so on, in the days and weeks following the festival.

In August Sadie had a new and unique opportunity to take an architectural boat tour of Chicago with a couple dozen of her closest friends. Now, I ask you, how many dogs, able-bodied or otherwise, get to do cool things like that? This came about when BringFido.com, a website dedicated to helping people find pet-friendly hotels, restaurants, destinations, attractions, and other services, gave me a beautiful hardcover book I could use for fund-raising purposes.

Just thinking it would be a cute idea, I put a pair of reading glasses on Sadie, posed her in front of the book, then sent the photo to BringFido.com. I was so surprised when Melissa from BringFido wrote me back and said, "Sadie needs to feel the wind in her hair. Let's set up an excursion for Sadie on the *Seadog* at Navy Pier in Chicago."

I said to myself, "Well, okay! Sadie's been on a plane, but she's never been on a pleasure cruise before. Why not?" They offered us a choice of cruise options and we settled on the ninety-minute architectural cruise that went through the Chicago Locks and up the Chicago River, offering close-up views of famous landmarks such as the Tribune Building, the Willis Tower, Buckingham Fountain, and the Merchandise Mart.

We assembled a whole group of people, Team Sadie members, friends, fans, and supporters, and drove the two hours down to Chicago in a convoy of vehicles all sporting Wisconsin license plates. When we arrived at Seadog Cruises we were met with a chalkboard shaped like a dog with a message welcoming Sadie. The staff could not have been kinder as they helped us load Sadie's wagon onto the brightly colored, diesel-powered speedboat with the large open deck for prime sightseeing.

As we took off and motored down the winding Chicago River with the intense afternoon sun glinting off the tall, majestic skyscrapers, throwing dazzling patterns and colorful kaleidoscopes of light across the boat's crowded deck, I leaned over to Sadie in her wagon beside me. "You are *my* sea dog," I said, stroking her head and scratching her ears. "You are my sky dog. You are my do-everything-and-make-it-amazing dog. How can I ever thank you for giving me my amazing life? How can I ever pay you back for what you've given me?"

Sadie, who'd been sitting up and eagerly watching the

towering buildings passing by, turned to me and rested her chin on my arm. "No worries, Mom," she seemed to be saying. "We love each other, and we are in this together."

As the year wound down, I took some time over Thanksgiving to step away from the twenty-four/seven whirlwind that was Saving Sadie to sit down and write a heartfelt holiday message to all our family, friends, supporters, and friends. I was having the most amazing, extraordinary, exciting, fulfilling time of my life, but I knew these things didn't happen in a vacuum. It took so many people and such commitment to keep Sadie and me going, which was what ultimately inspired me to get my thoughts down on paper and have Valerie post it on our website for everyone to see.

> To all of you who believe in Sadie,
> As Sadie's mom, there isn't a day that passes that I don't think about the wonder of YOU. If it weren't for YOU, Sadie wouldn't be here and the world would be a sadder, smaller place. I THANK YOU for all of your thoughts, support, and taking a chance on her so that Sadie can have a great quality of life. I wish that Sadie could meet each of you and give you a kiss or a paw press for all of your generosity. It took all of you to make Sadie what she is now, and Sadie and I thank you for making a commitment to help, in your own way, a very special animal.
> Sadie savors life every day and she never ceases to amaze me. From staring out the car window watching everything breeze by, to rolling in the snow and making a snack out of it with great big chomps, to "walk-

ing" to the gazebo in the yard, which is Sadie's favorite place, to flying down the stairs to score some cat food, Sadie loves every minute of every single day and her constant tail wagging tells me so.

This Thanksgiving, remember that Sadie and I love you so very much and we thank you for giving this incredible animal a second chance at life. Please appreciate the ones that surround you this holiday season (human and animal) and we will say a prayer of thanks for all of you beautiful humans who have helped make Sadie the joyful, playful creature that she is today.

Don't Stop Believin'.

With much love and doggie kisses,
Joal & Sadie

CHAPTER FOURTEEN

Pure Love and
Second Chances

Sadie teaching "Animals in the Media" at the University of Wisconsin-Milwaukee.

As time passed, Sadie grew from strength to strength as we continued developing our program and expanding our outreach to schools, libraries, community centers, and nursing homes. At the same time, we were also pursuing opportunities in larger, more diverse, and more challenging environments. For example, Sadie entered the sacred towers of academia when she presented a one-day session called Animals in the Media at the University of Wisconsin-Milwaukee, where she received her "dogtorate" from Joette Rockow, who was the course instructor. A few days later she appeared at the Toastmasters International convention at the Crown Plaza Airport in Milwaukee, where she had her own room for a meet-and-greet.

One of the really exciting developments during this time period was our growing involvement with the anti-bullying movement, particularly with the local group GAB—Generations Against Bullying. Our message to schoolchildren had always centered around disability acceptance and overcoming obstacles, as typified by our catchphrase, "Think about what you can do, not what you can't do—just like Sadie does."

This created a natural pathway for us to do a number of public appearances under the GAB umbrella, even while I maintained autonomy in my own slate of Sadie presentations and activities. GAB encouraged children not to be bystanders when other children or animals were being abused or bullied, but instead to be "upstanders" who stand up to the bullies and go to get help. When Sadie and I spoke at GAB events, I explained that the men who shot Sadie were the bullies while the people who came to rescue her were the upstanders.

Joining forces with GAB allowed us to expand our horizons in ways that otherwise would not have been possible. For example, in 2015 we took part in a GAB event with former Green Bay Packers star fullback William Henderson in which we visited ten schools in two days throughout the Kenosha Unified School District, talking to kids about bullying. The program was slightly different at every school, but in every case, Sadie and I were the last of the presenters to appear and the last to speak.

We had learned from previous experience that once kids saw Sadie, all their attention was immediately riveted to the dog, and nothing anyone else had to say would sink in. So during this whistle stop tour, Sadie and I, with her in her wagon, would hide out in the principal's office until we received the signal that they were ready for us. Then I would wheel out Sadie in her specially blinged-out wagon with a dramatic flourish, and the kids simply went crazy.

"Now, if you will all sit quietly and listen, you can all come up and meet Sadie and pet her when we are done," I explained. And with that, suddenly the kids became so quiet that you could hear a pin drop. At the end of the program, I invited all the kids to come forward to meet Sadie, who gladly (and patiently) welcomed her adoring fans.

*   *   *

Sadie continued to improve physically and mentally as a result of all our work with her. Sometimes progress was slow, especially in the area of nerve regeneration, but it was present. She was not walking, but she was "mobile," to some extent, preferring to be out of the wagon and moving on her own when we were at home. She could get around the house quite well, and when I let her outside she loved to go to the gazebo, where she could lounge in the grass, watch the birds and squirrels and rabbits, and feel the gentle breeze ruffling her fur.

In September 2015 Sadie experienced a major breakthrough in her rehab when she regained feeling in the bottom of her feet and was able to start getting out of the swimming pool on her own! The vets at the University of Wisconsin hospital had written in their report back in October 2013 that Sadie would never walk again and never be able to feel her feet. As she had done so many times before, Sadie proved the experts wrong! I knew that this did not guarantee that she'd ever be fully walking again, but it showed that improvement in her condition was still possible, even several years after she'd been shot, and that she was always able to beat the odds.

Sadie's treatment, therapy, and exercise regimen continued in earnest, with slightly different schedules depending on the time of year. In winter she got acupuncture with Dr. Jodie once a week and swam indoors at Think Pawsitive twice a week. After swimming she would spend time in the Soqi HotHouse machine beneath the far infrared rays. While in the HotHouse she would receive e-stim or Russian e-stim for twenty or thirty minutes on each side.

Russian e-stim was similar to the e-stim I had been doing myself on Sadie at home with the handheld device, but the Russian e-stim was more intense and set at a different frequency. We started working with Bill Anderson at Attitude Sports and he used a heavy-duty e-stim machine on Sadie, which seemed to produce an even greater effect. I knew that the vets at the UW Veterinary Hospital had said that e-stim and similar treatments were unlikely to benefit Sadie in any way, but we were seeing real progress from Sadie, and so I felt that there was no reason not to continue.

On other days we worked with Sadie in her leg braces, tempting her to take steps by using frozen peanut butter on a spoon or canned cat food. We also practiced her going up the stairs with the braces on her legs. Following that she would go for a five-minute spin on the Power Plate.

Sadie was also still getting her twenty-five pills and supplements twice a day and maintained her raw food diet. She never had to go back to doggy diapers and continued to be successful in urinating and detoxing on her own.

In summer Sadie's schedule featured a lot more swimming, often swimming every day at Jeff's pool. We had started using small weights on Sadie's legs when she was in the pool to further build her muscles. Our friend Kathy Boneck even fashioned her some custom-made weight holders out of cloth with pockets and Velcro, to wrap around her legs and place the small weights (like a metal washer) inside. We were gradually building up the amount of weight we used on her legs, and building up her time swimming with the weights to thirty minutes a session.

Her summer regimen also included a minimal amount of Power Plate, some e-stim, and at-home massage, along with stretching and chair exercises. Sadie amazed us all when this supposedly paralyzed dog started doing "high tens" thanks in part to Doc Clark at Synergy Works, double-bouncing on the ground and raising her front legs all the way above her head. Remarkable!

Kim Becker continued working with Sadie as her schedule allowed, on games and tasks designed to stretch Sadie's mind as much as her body. Kim's partner, Mary, also fell in love with Sadie and became a valuable member of the team. Mary made Sadie a beautiful handcrafted wooden board so that Sadie could exercise on it with her leg weights on in winter when it was too cold to swim.

The board was flat and was laid on two chairs positioned about four feet apart. Sadie was placed on the board with her front legs stretched out in front of her and her back legs dangling with the weights attached. This did wonders for Sadie's stretching and muscles building.

It was always remarkable to me to see how it wasn't just people Sadie met at events or out in public whom she quickly won over to her side; it was friends of family, and family of friends, and friends of friends. Sadie-love was contagious, but only in the best possible way.

Thinking about all of Sadie's therapies, exercises, and treatments, I realized that there were some people who questioned and criticized me for pouring so much time, money, and energy into saving Sadie and working to get her walking again when there were so many other worthy causes in the world.

I understood why people might say that. We are all touched by images of starving children, and we all know people who have died of cancer and diabetes and other horrible diseases. But it wasn't that I thought Sadie was more important than all those other worthy causes; it was that she was more important to me. Sadie is like my child—and ask any parent what he or she would do for their paralyzed child.

I would also explain to those who question Saving Sadie that Sadie has served as a kind of guinea pig in ways that might benefit many other animals and even people in the long run. Many of the therapies, treatments, exercises, and procedures that we've tried with Sadie have never been tried on a paralyzed dog before. What the vets and techs and others have learned from Sadie's experiences is being used to advance and refine new treatments and protocols that may even have applications for paralyzed humans sometime down the road.

When I think about all the ways that Sadie has changed me, and how my life has evolved since our paths first crossed, I am astonished. I don't feel that what I've done with Sadie is noble in any way; I set out to save one badly broken dog, not save the world. And in the end, the greatest change has been the change inside myself: I am the one who has truly been saved, not Sadie.

But even so, my journey with Sadie hasn't been without some setbacks and sorrows. I'm sorry to say that my family still isn't as accepting of Sadie as I wish they would be. I'm not sure what it will take to make that happen; with all that Sadie has accomplished in four short years, all the obstacles she has overcome, all the ways she has inspired adults and children with disabilities and special needs, perhaps there is nothing that will change my family's minds. And yet I choose to live in hope; hope is always an option, no matter the circumstances.

I know my devotion to Sadie has cost me in terms of other relationships, too. Caring for a disabled dog is in many ways similar to being the single parent of a toddler, but a toddler who never grows up and who will always need full-time care. And yet the massive number of people who have been helpful, who have given and cared and sacrificed in order to join Team Sadie, far outnumbers the very few who have not.

In addition to a few lost friends and relationships, I've missed out on other opportunities, too. For example, I had a chance to go to Europe last year but I turned it down rather than being so far away from Sadie and for so long. Some people might view this as a sacrifice, but I don't. What I've given up to care for her is minuscule compared to what I've gained.

And what I have gained is so significant and so wonderful. For example, my sister Marnette and I are now closer than ever before thanks to Sadie. The bond we forged in those early days of Saving Sadie will strengthen the connection between us forever.

I've also had the chance to experience the kindness and generosity of people, often total strangers, firsthand. I have met literally thousands of people that I couldn't have met any other way. Many of these people give me goose bumps, their stories touch me right down to my soul, especially when I see people from so many different walks of life being so kind and gentle with Sadie. Often the poorer someone is, the more he or she wants to help Sadie. I'll never forget the lady who cleaned college dorm rooms for a living and had three kids to feed and still she gave five dollars for Sadie's care.

I've witnessed grown men and women start to weep when I tell them Sadie's story, and then I have also seen those tears of sorrow turn into tears of joy when I explain that Sadie's story isn't ultimately a sad story, it's a story of triumph, it's a story of pure love and second chances.

At a time in my life when I least expected it, when I thought I was winding down and that life's greatest joys were likely behind me, Sadie gave me a new and unexpected purpose in life. Suddenly I had a mission to accomplish, a mission that would introduce me to people I never would have met and take me to places I never could have imagined.

Ultimately, what I am left with is that Sadie has taught me a different way to love, a way that is simpler, more basic, more holy; it is more sacred and more spiritual than ordinary, everyday love can ever be. She has taught me to love without expectation, without condition, to love in uncertainty, and with no promise of return. In other words, Sadie has shown me the purest and most perfect love there is.

Thank you, Sadie, for choosing me to be your mom. Thank you for allowing me to be part of your journey. The rest of the world mistakenly believes that I saved you, but really, the reverse is true. You saved me, and I love you more than you can ever imagine. I can't wait to see what the next part of our journey will bring.

ACKNOWLEDGMENTS

Of all the countless individuals who helped make this book happen, the authors would especially like to thank Marnette Bowen for all her connections and her help with photos, details, and documents; Valerie Alba for help with photos and her social media expertise; and Jeff Ziglinski for taking expert care of Sadie, Sparky, Miss Kitty, and Kitty Kat while Mommy was busy writing. Thanks to our agent, Barbara Ellis of Scribes Literary & Editorial, and our editor, Michaela Hamilton at Kensington, for taking a chance on us and believing in Sadie's story.

Elizabeth would especially like to thank her feline housemates, Claudius and Calpurnia, for granting her permission to work on a "dog book." She looks forward to earning back their love sometime in the near future.

Joal would like to give special thanks to Sparky, Miss Kitty, and Kit Kat, for welcoming Sadie into the family and for their understanding and realizing Sadie needed extra care. Thank you, Sadie, for saving me, and for choosing me as your mother.

*The authors would also like to thank the
following individuals and organizations for
their support of Sadie and for their assistance in making
this book happen.*

Beth Abyss, Deanna Adam, Mary Albanesi, Joseph Amato, Gary Antol, Dianna Armstrong-Bickett, Nadia Aronson, Michele Artascos, Brigit Asilnejad, James Atten, Joseph and Christine Aufiero

Dr. Diane Baehr, Lucinda Bain, Sharon Baines, Deborah Baldwin, Tamas Balint, William Ball, Melanie Balzer, Andy & Stephan Bandy, Alison Barratt, Charlene Batson, Tracy Beck, Kim Becker, Martina Bernini, Jim Berscheid, Haly Besaw, Peter Best, Susan Bett, Cheri Beverly, Susan Biglovsky, Neil Bissex, Basha Blades, Shannon Blankenship, Lauren Bloom, John and Janis Bolskar, Kathy Bonek, Chandra Bonfiglio, Garrett and Michelle Borden, Kerah Botham, Mari Bowman, Melissa Boxx, Donna Bradley, Terrill Brandon, Dean Bravo, Helen Briner, Christopher Brown, Kevin Brown, Steve Brown, W.H. Brown, Meredith Bruder, Matthew Bruno, Mr. and Mrs. Bruning, Carol Budney, Breanna Bukowski, Audrey Burch, Margaret Burke, Linda Burkhead, Thomas Burnett, Lynn Busch, Tana Buss, Rondi Bussey, Gerald Buster

Haley Caddell, Cynthia Callewaert, John Cameron, Kathie Carestia, James and Holly Carlini, Debbie and Begley Carls, Barbara Cappelli, Jay Carr, Sharon Carrier, Priscilla Carton, Shelia Casey, Robert and Dianne Castellini, Fatima Catena, Dr. Adam Chaifetz, Cece Chavez, Kathy Chiavola, Jenica Childs, Joseph Chin, Carol Ciana, Joan Ciapas, Julie Ciapas, Frances Cimino, Doc Clark, Susan Clayton, Heather Cobban, Bobbie Cohen, Kathleen Colbert, Zoraida Colon,

Steve Comeau, Joyce Conner, Jewel Conover, Burt
Constable, Karin Conway, Carole Cook, Jackie Cook,
Brogna Cordasco Giovanna, Shelley Corley Grubbs, Barbara
Corn, John Cook, Nancy Correa, Karen Cox, Lisa Craycraft,
Jenefer Creamer, Jill Cresko, Ann Crosby, M.P. Cupentino,
Daniel and Michelle Czerwinski

Patty DaPonte, Ingrid Davidson, Cynthia Davis, Keri Davis,
Timothy Davis, Margaret Davison, Rosemary Day, James
Dean, Jennifer Deangelo, Brooke Dehart, Clairone Delaney,
Kara DeLarco, Kristin Deluca, Dr. Jami Derse, Steven
Destrampe, Janet Dewitt, Geraldine Dierks, Queade Di Ilio,
David Dodenhoff, Debbie Theodore Dogstuff, Bob and
Dona Doig, Kathryn Doig, Maria Donnelly, Janet Dorak,
Joanne Douglas, Helen Dowzall, Jessica Dragan, Joe Drantz,
Gregg Dries

William Eaves, Joan Eberhardt, Carol Edwards, Sarah Egea,
Cheryl Eggar, Daniela Eguizabal, Gabriella Eguizabal, Bill
Eisner, Linda Ellerton, Mary Ellis, Cate Elsten, Lorraine
Emerick, Janice Erickson, Susan Estright, Cathy Evans,
Shannon Evans, Dr. Leslie Evelo

Stephanie Falcone, Terri Fancher, Brittany Farina,
Steve Fawthrop, Dorothy Fegan, Judith Felsmann, Deborah
Finke, Robb Fischer, Paula Forassiepi, Marilynn Ford, Alice
Forest, John Fox, Louise Foxe, Caroline Farquhar, Frank
Fredenburg, Angel Frcc, Paula and Harry Frey, Andrea
Friedland, Deb Fries, Kathie Fritzen, Cynthia Fusco

Jone Gagnon, Tara Gamblen, Stockton Garver, Cathy Gault,
Lauren Gauthier, Jason George, Eric Gerber, Cynthia
Doucette Giacomini, Kathy Gibbons, Christopher Gibson,
Alison Gilbert, Kati Gingras, Lou Ann Giunta, Cynthia
Goehring, Lynn Goldberg, Mary Gordon, Charlie Gorney,

Philip Goodwin, Stephanie Graham, Barbara Green, Linda Green, Anita Gregorian, Jon Grider, Kathleen Groeger, Michelle Gulliver

Marian Hailey-Moss, Terry Haire, Susan Haisty, Rita Hale, Claudia Hall, Charmaine Hammond, Judith Hansell, Pamela Hansen, Sherry Hanson, Karyn Harden, Tricia Harrington, Rita Hale, Jacquelyn Hawley, Elizabeth Haynes, Alice Hecht-Soliman, Alan Hefter, Andrew and Kerry Heistad, Sonia Heller Schulthess, Rhonda Hemming, Gm Hendershot, Linda Hendrickson, Carolyn Hennesy, Jack Herbert, Tom Heron, Donna Hess, Maximillian Hess, Dianna Higgins, Robert Hill, Sharon Hite, Sarah Hoff, Linda Hoffpauir, Maxine Hollfelder, Cara Hoppen, Steve and Sandra Horowitz, Patricia Hubbard, Deni Huffman, Craig Hunkins, Bethany Hunt, Jo Hupperich

Dee Ilyas, Barbara Ingle, Victoria Ivashkova, Kathy Iverson

Kathryn Jablonsky, Linda Jackson, Sharylla Jackson, Shannon Jacobs, Doris Jacomet, Sara Janey, Daisy Jassar, Douglas Javier, Judith Jerominski, Doug Jimenez, Kent Johansen, Judy Johnsen, Callia Johnson, Dave Johnson, David N. Johnson, Marty Johnson, Judith Johnson, K. Johnson, Laura Johnson, Dave and Pat Johnson-Dorow, Lloyd Johnston, Carol S. Jones

Christine Kaahui-Estrada, Cliff and Elaine Kaclow, Amy Kamedulski, Joi Kamper, Jo and Miranda Kapfhammer, Elaine Karasch, Mike Kass, Stan Kass, Sandra Kassulke, Inga Katelari, Meridena Kauffman, Antoinette Kean, Kathleen Kearns, Nancy Kelley, Robi Kelly, Beatrice Kemp, Brandt Kennedy, Rebecca Kimsey, Sharon Klein, Jennifer Kolesar, Fran Kolpack, Denise Konkol, Elaine Konitzer, Christine

Koss, Alice Kotsakis, Jennifer Kovacich, Larry & Nancy Kremer, Ann Marie Krok, Jennifer Krouchick, Dr. Tammy Krukowski, Thomas and Janet Krumplitsch, Stacy Krygier, Renee Kryston, Amanda Kryzanowski

Brad & Cindy Laatsch, Michele Lail, Marilynn Lalobas, David Land, Debbie Landers, Julie Lane, Desmond & Jeanne LaPlace, Karenlu Lapolice, Judith Larsen, Mary Laub, Tammy Laub, Brenda Lauer, Selena Lauterer, Julie Lawell, Phil and Andi LeBoy, Linda Lee, Brian Leitzke, Jessie Lendennie, Carole Leonard, Craig Lesser, Judy Levshakoff, Mark Liccione, Widge Liccione, Carol and Robert Linville, Carolyn Lombardi, Carolyn Long, Randy Lorenz, Marilyn Loveless, Lyn D. Loven, Maureen Lughart, Susan Lygo, Nancy Lyon-Gray

Denise MacLeod, Christine Magri, Lee Mallatratt, David Maller, Marisa Malone, Deborah Mann, Arthur March, Dr. Paddy Mark, Colleen Marko, Bruce Marks, Caitlin Marmion, Caitlin Marms, Mary Marshall, Christine Martello, Susan Mathis, Mary Martorana, Lorraine Matarese, Veronica Mather, John Matsis, Cody Matthews, Dobie Maxwell, Deane Mazur, Victoria Mazzotta, Patricia McCaffrey, Claire McDougal, Sherry McKinney, Molly McKnight, Scott McLeod, Tina McNeil, Lisa and Tom McNeill, Lorraine Mechem, Marilyn Mee, Grace Melby, Sue Meng, David Meros, Donna Mersing, Janice Meyer, Andera Meyers, Jodee Michell, Martine Michelle, Mm. Mielke, Dan Mikulecky, Regina Milano, Pat and Mike Milkowski, Diane Millard, Sarah Millard, Bernadette Miller, Elaine Mills, Denise Mitchell, Tracie Mitchum, Melissa Moericke, Shane Morris, Shelia Moulder, Martha Munoz, Vicki Murley, Anne Murphy, Brenda Musson, Sheila Moulder, Senara Mulitalo

Agnes Nelson, Sandy Nichols, William Nicholson, Irene Niles, Cynthia Novitsky, Sharon Norber, Mercedes Nunez Mendez

Cathe Odom, Todd Oilschlager, Margaret O'Kelley, Lydia Oliver, Leslie O'Loughlin, James and Megan Olszewski, Raundi O'Neil-Jones, John Opsitnick, Colleen Oreskovich, Jay Ormsby, Harry Osborne

Toni Pabon, Robert Page, Debra Parkes Devlin, Laura Patterson, Randy Pauls, Mary Pearce, Laura Peirano, Pat Peterson, Donald Petzold, Jaclyn Phillips, Melonie Plimpton, Christina Ponder, Peter Pope, J. M. Prasczewicz, Kathleen Prazenka, Nan Preussler, Jeanni Price, Melissa Price, Raine Prinzivalle, I. Pronker-Haveman, Patricia Pruss

Sandra Quelch, Amalia Quinlan

Robert Rach, Janet Raede Witt, Whitney Rainero, Noreen Rapp, Amy Rasmussen, Elizabeth Ratke, Barbara Rawson, Diane Rector, Frances Redick, Nicole Redmann, Jane Reeves, Manuela Ribeiro, Diane Richards, Basha Richey, Rhonda Ricker, Jane Rider, Chief Joe Rieder, Cheri Riehle, Robert Ritholz, Ann Roberts, the Robinials, Carolyn Robinson, Joyce Robinson, Susan Robinson, Trai Rochon, Joette Rockow, Jessica Rodriguez, Charlene Romer, Todd Rongstad, Tedford Rose, Ellen Rosoff, Marsha Ross, Pauline Rossen, Wanda Roth, Marilyn Rothfelder, Pam Rouda, Mike Rozumalski, Elke Rudloff DVM, DAC, VECC, Shelly Runte, Kitty Russell, Anne Rutger Neafie, Arleen Rutten, Mary Rynders

Sasha Sabbeth, Nancie Sailor, Aja Saler, Virginia Savio, Joseph Sawicki, Marcia Scattergood, Tracy Scheinoha, Arlene Schmidt, Karen Schmocker, Jay Schroeder, Mary Schultz,

Joan Schweickert, Jenny Schwiner, David and Christine Seidman, Jeanne Sexton, the Shaffers, Melinda Shaw, Robert and Roberta Shaw, Kama Sherpa, Tedarat Shufflebarger, Pat Sidello, Karen Siegel, Olivia Silensky, Charlotte Simkins, Laura Simpson, Linda Sipek, Angela Slawny, Stuart Slom, Carol Smetts, Jenny Smiley, Annetta Smith, Kent and Dorothy Smith, Margaret Soden, Maria Solis, Scott Solomon, Shirley Sonnichsen, Jami Sotonoff, Dr. Joel Spatt, Robin Spencer, Cathy Spyres, Natalia Stadelbauer, Bob Stankus, Mary Stanley, Becky Starr, Carol Lynn Stempler, Marcy Stephens, RN, Anne Stephenson, Timothy and Lori Stern, Judith Stevely, David Stewart, Jean Stewart, Melanie Stillfried, Sue Stirzaker, Suan Strawman, Glenn and Kristina Strozewski, Lori Strunk, Webster Strunk, Keith Sudano, Manussawee Sukunta, Joe Sullivan, Mariana Suman, Bryan Summers, Gregg and Sally Sustache, Dennis Sutton, Brendan Sweeney, Jonathan Synovic, Jim and Lynda Szczepanik

Kathryn Tacadena, Olivia Tan, Jessica Taske, David Tauke, David and Judy Taylor, Jack Taylor, Barbara Techel, Debbie Theodore, Karen Thomas, Marsha Thompson, Susan Tillman, William Tilton, Lori Tkach, Robert Tollemeo, Jane Toth-Barton, Patricia Towers, Diana Traegler, Jaclyn Trevillian, Patti Triola, Anita Tully, Barbara Tunick

Amy & Juliana Udoni

Mark Van Vehel, Debra Velie, Rui Viegas, Doreen Virtue, Asia Voight, Deborah Voves

Deb Wadkins, Sarah Wages, Rosemary Wagley, Patricia Wagner, Louise Walsh, Jeanne Walters, Stephanie Warren, Mary Watkins, Lynda Wawryk, Lisa Weaver, Dr. Barbara Weber, Louis Weisberg, Bonnie Welch, Kenneth Wentland,

Vickie West, Richard Westlein, Derek Wharton, Joe Wiggins, Joanie Wilcox, Terry Wilde, Kathy Wilson, Laura Wilson, William and Diane Wilson, Linda Winfrey, Chuck Wiseman, William Witherup, Donna Wolden, Lori Wolff, Beth Woolsey, Linda Worrell, Gypsy Wulff

Sheryl Young, Marianne Young Bowman

Mary Lynn Zahn, Gwen and Allen Zajac, Sarah Zaug, Gregory & Marlene Zautke, Alissa Zea, Dustin Zick

Companies

Acres of Hope and Aspirations, www.acresofhopeandaspirations.org
Action Graphics
Alta Reserve
Animal Doctor Holistic Veterinary Complex, www.animaldoctormuskego.com
The Animal Medical Care Foundation, www.animalmedicalcarefoundation.com
Animal Wellness Center, www.awcwi.com
Animal Wellness magazine, www.animalwellnessmagazine.com
Asia Voight, www.asiavoight.com
Attitude Sports, www.attitudesports.com
Author Gypsy Wulff, www.authorgypsywulff.wordpress.com

Bark 'n Scratch Outpost, www.milwaukeepetfood.com
Best Friends, bestfriends.org
Bosco's Social Club, www.facebook.com/boscosbar
Bottles 'n Brushes, www.bottlesnbrushes.com

Care2, www.care2.com

Clear Channel, www.iheartmedia.com/Pages/Home.aspx

Charmaine Hammond, www.charmainehammond.com

Core Expression

Creatures Covers, www.creaturescovers.com

Crystal Carolina Canine Rehabilitation,
www.manta.com/c/mt5x31k/crystal-carolina-canine-rehab

Daily Herald, www.dailyherald.com

Dawgs in Motion, dawgsinmotion.com

Dobie Maxwell, dobiemaxwell.com

Dogster magazine, www.dogster.com

Doig Corporation, doigcorp.com

Earthborn Holistic, www.earthbornholisticpetfood.com

Eddie's Wheels, eddieswheels.com

Epic Web Design

Feline Freedom Coalition, www.felinefreedom.org

Fox6 News, fox6now.com

GAB: Generations Against Bullying, www.gabnow.org

GEO Investment Group LLC

GooFurr, goofurr.com

Hamburger Mary's Bar & Grille,
www.hamburgermarys.com

The Harmony Fund/The Great Animal Rescue,
www.harmonyfund.org

Heritage Ballet

The Horizon Group

Horny Goat Brewing Company,
www.hornygoatbrewco.com

iPAW: Integrating People for Animal Wellness,
www.ipawaid.com

Joyful Paws, joyfulpaws.com

Kayla's Krew, www.kaylaskrew.org/index.html
Kim's Costumes, www.kimscostumeshop.com
Kountry Krafts

Lakeshore Veterinary Specialists,
www.lakeshorevetspecialists.com
Landmark Credit Union, www.landmarkcu.com
The Lovin' Oven Pet Bakery,
www.thelovinovenpetbakery.com
LSR Technology LLC, www.lsr.com

Marquette University, www.marquette.edu
Milwaukee County Office of the Sheriff,
county.milwaukee.gov/OfficeoftheSheriff7719.htm
Moose Mountain Lodge
City of Muskego Police Department,
www.cityofmuskego.org/police
Mystic Ireland, LLC, www.mysticirelandusa.com

Noah's Arks Rescue, www.noahs-arks.net
Nonbox, nonbox.com

Pam's Paws, www.facebook.com/Pams-Paws-
370506216371051/
Pawz Dog Boots, www.pawzdogboots.com
Paws to Embrace, Therapy Dogs,
www.facebook.com/PawstoEmbraceTherapyDogs/
Pet Helpers, pethelpers.org
Petlicious Dog Bakery & Pet Spa, www.petlicious.com
Pet Supplies 'N' More, petsupplies-n-more.com
Pet World Warehouse, petworldoutlet.com
Pewaukee Veterinary Service, pewaukeeveterinary
service.com

Redstone Media Group, www.redstonemediagroup.com
Rita Hale, Bemer Group, www.ritahale.bemergroup.com
Rustico Pizza

Sacred Kinship, www.sacredkinship.com
Save Our Strays
Source 1, www.source1parts.com
Speed Staffing LLC, www.facebook.com/
Speed-Staffing-LLC-515742928454746/
Spiral Café
Spiral I
SpiritWings Publications, spiritwingspubs.com.au
Starfish Animal Rescue, www.starfishanimalrescue.com
Stubby's Gastrogrub & Beer Bar, stubbyspubandgrub.com
Studio 951
Synergy Works

Team Toby, theoriginalteamtoby.hammondgroup.biz/
Think Pawsitive, thinkpawsitivedog.com
Today's TMJ4, www.tmj4.com
TOPS Veterinary Rehabilitation, www.tops-vet-rehab.com
Treasures A-Z, treasuresaz.com
Trees of Hope, WI, www.treesofhopewi.org
Turning Points in Compassion, turningpointsin
compassion.info/#home

Urban Ecology Center, urbanecologycenter.org

Valerie L. Alba Virtual Assistance LLC, vlasupervallc.com
Veterinary Housecall Care, LLC, veterinaryhouse
callcare.com

Whispering Oats Farms,
www.motorcarriersalliance.org/350909/whispering-oats-
farms-inc

Whitewater Police Department, www.whitewater-wi.gov/department/police

Winston's Wishes, www.facebook.com/winstonswishes/

Wisconsin Gazette,wisconsingazette.com

Wisconsin Wellness Clinic, www.wisconsinwellnessclinic.com

WISN, www.wisn.com

WKLH, wklh.com

Zen Yoga Reiki, zenyogareiki.com

For more information about Sadie

www.savingsadie.com
www.savingsadiemovie.com
www.facebook.com/SavingSadie
twitter.com/SavinSadie
www.youtube.com/user/SaveSadieNow
www.pinterest.com/SavinSadie/
www.tumblr.com/blog/savingsadie
www.instagram.com/savinsadie/
www.thumbtack.com/wi/muskego/presentation-design/animal-personal-appearances